1996

an introduction to

HELPING ADULTS

LEARN

W9-DGV-626

and

CHANGE

by

Russell D. Robinson, Ph.D.

Professor of Adult Education
University of Wisconsin—Milwaukee

Revised Edition

OMNIBOOK CO.
1171 Decorah Road
West Bend, Wisconsin 53095
Phone: (414) 675-2760   FAX: (414) 675-2340

> To learn is to change. Education is a process that changes the learner.
>
> — *George Leonard*

> He who's not busy being born is busy dying.
>
> — *Bob Dylan*

> Except a man be born again, he cannot see the kingdom of God.
>
> — *Christ Jesus*

> It is not unusual to find that major changes in life. . .break the patterns of our lives and reveal to us quite suddenly how much we had been imprisoned by the comfortable web we had woven around ourselves. Unlike the jailbird, we don't know that we've been imprisoned until after we've broken out.
>
> —*John W. Gardner*

> This life, therefore, is not righteousness but growth in righteousness, not health but healing, not being but becoming, not rest but exercise. We are not yet what we shall be, but we are growing toward it. The process is not yet finished, but it is going on. This is not the end, but it is the road. All does not gleam in glory, but all is being purified.
>
> —*Martin Luther*

> *The awareness of anomaly opens a period in which conceptual categories are adjusted until the initially anomalous has become the anticipated. At this point the discovery has been completed.*
> —*Thomas S. Kuhn*

> *There is only one good, knowledge, and one evil, ignorance.*
> —*Socrates*

> *Learning without thought is labor lost; thought without learning is perilous.*
> —*Confucius*

> *Nothing ever becomes real till it is experienced — even a proverb is no proverb to you till your Life has illustrated it.*
> —*John Keats*

to my mother,

> *Dorothea Carter Robinson,*
> *example of life-long learning,*
> *for whom each life experience was another opportunity to learn.*

to my children,

> *my daughter, Lynn,*
> *and my sons, Daniel and Dean,*
> *for whom continuing education is the door and the path*
> *to lifetimes of adventure unlimited.*

to my grandchildren,

> *Steven, Heather, Jennifer, and Brittany,*
> *who are beginning their journeys.*

and to my wife, Helen,

> *partner, helper, learner, changer, friend.*

> *It is high time we freed ourselves of attachments to old forms and eased the flight of the unfettered human mind.*
>
> —*Marilyn Ferguson*

> *The life which is unexamined is not worth living.*
>
> —*Plato*

> *Towering genius disdains a beaten path. It seeks regions hitherto unexplored.*
>
> —*Abraham Lincoln*

> *They (the Americans) have all a lively faith in the perfectibility of man; they judge that the diffusion of knowledge must necessarily be advantageous, and the consequences of ignorance fatal; they all consider society as a body in a state of improvement, humanity as a changing scene, in which nothing is, or ought to be, permanent; and they admit that what appears to them today to be good, may be superseded by something better tomorrow.*
>
> —*Alexis de Tocqueville*

CONTENTS
helping adults learn and change

.0 DEVELOPING TEACHING PLANS
Sequencing and Selecting

.1 TECHNIQUES AND DEVICES
Variety and Appropriateness

.2 CONDUCTING EVALUATION
Instructional Improvement

.3 ADULT EDUCATION
Study and Practice

OVERVIEW
A Model of Adult Education

BIBLIOGRAPHY
References for Further Study

INDEXES

> "Adult education includes all the activities with an educational purpose that are carried on by the people in the ordinary business of life."
> —Lyman Bryson, Columbia University, 1936

> "Adult education is the activity by which a mature person attempts to improve himself by adding to his skills or knowledge, developing his insights or his appreciation, or changing his attitudes; or the activity of individuals and agencies to change mature people in these ways."
> —Cyril O. Houle, University of Chicago, 1959

> "The term adult education is used to designate all those educational activities that are designed specifically for adults. . . .Whatever the form, content, duration, physical setting, or sponsorship, an activity is identified as adult education when it is part of a systematic, planned, instructional program for adults."
> —Coolie Verner, University of British Columbia, 1964

INTRODUCTORY NOTE

This book is about helping. Helping adults learn and change, particularly helping adults who help adults learn and change. There are many such helpers: teachers, consultants, administrators, programmers, managers, supervisors, trainers, counselors and the list goes on, literally millions of adults engaged daily in some form of facilitating adult learning, helping adults learn and change. Most of these practicing adult educators may not even think of themselves as adult educators. Yet that is what they are. This book provides a convenient collection of useful material, and opens the door to additional self-instruction listing on each page suggested "further study references" citing one or more of the 338 books listed in the bibliography.

Conducting one, two, and three-day workshops for adult educators on such topics as adult learning, change, adult development, motivation, teaching methods, communication and program planning, I early became acutely aware of the need for a concise publication that could be put in the hands of workshop participants. This led to the first edition of this book in 1979, and later minor revisions with subsequent printings. The time has come for a thoroughgoing revision. More than 30 additional pages of material not included in the earlier edition have been incorporated. Almost no page has been left untouched. Some 159 titles have been added to the bibliography, virtually all published since the first edition of this book.

This revised edition maintains the features and format that made the earlier versions useful for so many teachers of adults throughout the United States and Canada. This book brings together, in one publication, subject matter that might otherwise require a dozen or more books to provide. In outline form, suitable for workshops, I have collected a substantial amount of basic material useful to the practitioner of adult education. Where I have drawn heavily from a particular writer or theorist I have indicated the author in the text. Some application worksheets are also included which can be used in workshop settings or by individual readers for self-instruction.

A single workshop (or whole semester course for that matter) can provide only an introduction to what one needs to know and do to be most effective in helping adults learn and change. But the insights gained, combined with persistent application and practice, can help any teacher or helper of adults continue to improve his/her understanding and skills in the facilitation of adult learning.

Russell D. Robinson

Milwaukee, 1994

"*The necessity for wise direction, assistance, and encouragement of full grown people's mature intellectual power and desire is as great as in the period of
youth and of school life. Therefore grown people need
courses of study outlined, books for reading indicated, questions answered, associations formed, and all
the conditions guaranteed which tend to promote
hope, confidence, ambition, and strong purpose.*"
—*John H. Vincent, founder of Chautauqua,*
1886

"*A fresh hope is astir. From many quarters comes the
call to a new kind of education with its initial
assumption affirming that education is life—not a
mere preparation for an unknown kind of future
living. . . . This new venture is called adult
education—not because it is confined to adults but
because adulthood, maturity, defines its limits.*"
—*Eduard Lindeman, 1926*

"*University Extension is meant for those for whom
religion is intended; for those for whom life, liberty,
and the pursuit of happiness is intended. It is meant
to help the ignorant who desire knowledge — that
they may learn wisely; to reveal to the half-educated
the insufficiency of their knowledge; to arouse intellectual sluggards; to stimulate those who are in
the right way; to bring questions to the hearts of the
self-satisfied.*"
—*American Society for the Extension of University
Teaching, 1910*

1 ADULT LEARNING
a matter of change

> "Learning is not a task. . .it is a way to be in the world. Man learns as he pursues goals and projects that have meaning for him."
> —Sidney Jourard

Adult Learning is Problem-centered

1. Purposeful learning occurs when individuals experience a problem or recognize a gap between where they are and where they want to be, and then institute a self-inquiry in which the learner draws on whatever resources are available (teacher, literature, one's own or another's experience) to acquire the learnings deemed necessary to close the gap. All education is self-education.

2. Belief that a learning experience will help an adult cope with problems becomes a powerful motivator for participation in adult education.

3. Youth education is largely subject-centered and future-oriented. Youths take "subjects" — all of which are supposed to be important or needed in the future. Adult education, on the other hand, is problem-centered. Adults insist that the learning have relevance and value now.

4. Youth education is generally compulsory, with youths having virtually no say in what they are supposed to learn. Adult education is essentially voluntary. Adults drop out of those educational situations that are not seen as helping them to cope. (That is also the reason youths drop out, either mentally or physically!)

5. The central organizing principle for adult education must be around problems adults face, not subject-matter. The fact is, most problems in life involve *several* subject matters impinging in one way or another on the problem the adult hopes to resolve.

   • Emphasis in courses, workshops, classes, meetings, must be on helping adults learn how to cope with their problems.

   • Therefore, the teacher must be more *person*-centered than subject-centered.

- Therefore, the institution must market and promote the educational activity on the basis of its utility: How will this help the learner?

  Example:
  Rather than courses in:
  Elementary Principles of Supervision
  Supervisory Theory and Practice
  Advanced Supervisory Techniques
  Courses are more likely to attract adults as:
  Getting Ready to be a Supervisor
  Dealing With the Daily Problems of a Supervisor
  Improving Your Ability to Help Subordinates Develop

6. Learning is a complex process. Each individual brings the whole self to the process, all of that person's own unique array of needs, perceptions, assumptions, emotions, interests, values, beliefs, and the whole of life experience.

7. Learning is an internal process that takes place in the learner and nowhere else.

> *"The pleasures arising from thinking and learning will make us think and learn all the more."*
> —*Aristotle*

Adults as Learners

1. What We Know About Adults *(adapted from Rosemary Caffarella)*

   - Adults can and do want to learn, regardless of their age.

   - For the most part, adults are pragmatic in their learning. They tend to want to apply their learning to present situations.

   - Adults come to a learning situation with their own personal goals and objectives, which may or may not be the same as those given for the learning situation.

   - Adults have a rich background of experience. They tend to learn best when new information builds on past knowledge and experience.

   - Adults are motivated to learn based on a combination of complex internal and external forces which tend to encourage and/or inhibit learning.

   - Adults appear to be better motivated to learn when they become actively involved in the learning process.

further study references: 45, 144, 173, 189, 210, 233, 241, 301, 330

- Adults learn best in situations that are both psychologically and physically comfortable.

- Most adults tend to hold perceptions of themselves as independent and self-reliant people.

- Adults have different levels and styles of learning.

- Much of the adult's learning tends to have an effect on others (work colleagues, family, friends, customers, clients, etc.).

All Learning Involves Change

1. Learning is not passive absorption, but an active process of translating new knowledge, insights, skills and values into one's conduct.

2. There is always some pain involved in giving up the ideas and ways of doing things with which one has become comfortable in favor of new ways of doing things. Therefore, learning is resisted — actively, subtly, and even unconsciously.

3. The learner must become dissatisfied enough with present performance to want to change, accept the fact that it is a difficult process which he/she will tend to resist, and analyze the forces within that are resisting change and honestly take steps to overcome them.

4. When the learner feels the need for change and yet wishes to maintain present attitudes and behavior, an ambivalence or conflict is set up between "the old" and "the new." We, as learners, may defend ourselves against ideas that force us to admit our limitations; we may resist the will of someone else or something else to change us. Our defense may take some of the following forms:

   - Projection — defending our present behavior by asserting ourselves as we now are and by blaming somebody or some circumstances.

   - Rationalization — finding reasons to justify our present feelings, opinions and behavior.

   - Resistance — becoming angry and withdrawing or not listening actively in order to protect ourselves.

5. The learner himself must make the decision to learn as he struggles with himself — the new way of thinking and feeling *vs.* his habitual ways. He can learn when he is free to face this ambivalence within himself in a climate where

   - No one insists on changing him.

   - He can express himself freely.

   - He feels accepted regardless of his attitude.

   - He is not attacked or put on the defensive as a person.

Purposes for Adult Learning

1. Personal Growth and Development (*Abraham Maslow, Carl Rogers, Malcolm Knowles, Leon McKenzie*)

    *   Purpose: individual self-actualization; Knowles says, "it gives precedence to growth of people over the accomplishment of things"

    *   Content: whatever promotes individual growth

    *   Instruction: focus on student needs, group interaction

2. Personal and Social Improvement (*John Dewey, Eduard Lindeman, Paul Bergevin, Kenneth Benne*)

    *   Purpose: dual function of personal development and social progress; Lindeman says of learners, "they will be as eager to improve their collective enterprises, their groups, as they are to improve themselves."

    *   Content: practical, drawn from life situations, emphasis on the individual within the social context

    *   Instruction: problem solving with teachers and learners as partners

3. Organizational Effectiveness (*Chris Argyris, Leonard Nadler*)

    *   Purpose: programs designed to achieve organizational goals through "human resource development"

    *   Content: drawn from "training needs" of "human capital" for both individual and organizational development

    *   Instruction: wide variety of instructional methods

4. Cultivation of the Intellect (*K. H. Lawson, R. W. K. Patterson*)

    *   Purpose: education, learning valued for its own sake; Patterson says purpose is to "transmit knowledge that is educationally worthwhile" and that is "morally, socially, and politically neutral"

    *   Content: liberal studies

    *   Instruction: traditional teacher to learner

further study references: 8, 10, 17, 19, 27, 168, 196, 219, 229, 250, 258, 272, 307

5.   Social Transformation (*Paulo Freire, Ivan Illich, Myles Horton*)

- Purpose: cause radical social change through adult education which challenges the social system and transforms and liberates

- Content: drawn from the consciousness of the oppressed and disadvantaged

- Instruction: teacher is also learner in dialogical encounter that leads to reflective thought and action

> "We need to dare extend the metaphor of self-healing to a global dimension and to change some of our self-limiting assumptions about the world, taking inspiration from the small successes we have experienced in our personal lives. This means . . . consciously testing out our own ability to make a difference, and knocking on some of the imaginary doors that we thought were shut against us."
> — *Peggy Taylor*

Some "Principles of Adult Learning"

1.   Learning is an active process and adults prefer to participate actively.

- Therefore, those techniques that make provision for active participation will achieve more learning faster than those that do not.

2.   Learning is goal-directed and adults are trying to achieve a goal or satisfy a need.

- Therefore, the clearer, the more realistic and relevant the statement of desired outcomes, the more learning that will take place.

3.   Group learning insofar as it creates a "learning atmosphere" of mutual support, may be more effective than individual learning.

- Therefore, those techniques based on group participation are often more effective than those which handle individuals as isolated units.

4.   Learning that is applied immediately is retained longer and is more subject to immediate use than that which is not.

- Therefore, techniques must be employed that encourage the immediate application of any material in a practical way.

5. Learning must be reinforced.

   • Therefore, techniques must be used that insure prompt, reinforcing feedback.

6. Learning new material is facilitated when it is related to what is already known.

   • Therefore, the techniques used should help the adult establish this relationship and integration of material.

7. The existence of periodic plateaus in the rate of learning necessitates frequent changes in the nature of the learning task to insure continuous progress.

   • Therefore, techniques should be changed frequently in any given session.

8. Learning is facilitated when the learner is aware of his progress.

   • Therefore, techniques should be used that provide opportunities for self-appraisal.

9. Learning is facilitated when there is a logic to the subject matter and the logic makes sense in relation to the learner's repertoire of experience.

   • Therefore, learning must be organized for sequence and cumulative effects.

Adult Learners in Learning Groups

1. Often adult learning takes place in groups — a classroom or learning group — where the learner can draw on the experience and organized knowledge of a teacher or leader and (ideally) others in the group. But it is well to remember that the "reason" an adult comes to a continuing education group setting may not be just what the teacher has in mind. Three motivational orientations of group-setting learners have been identified *(Cyril Houle)*:

   • *Goal-directed* learners who use education for accomplishing fairly clear-cut objectives.

   • The *activity-oriented,* (often socially motivated), who take part because they find in the circumstances of the learning a meaning which has no necessary connection with the content or announced purpose of the activity.

   • The *learning-oriented* who seek knowledge for its own sake.

2. Estimates indicate there are as many as 60 million adults in the United States engaged in some form of organized adult education, 46 million of them outside of the school and college systems.

3. In any case, there are more persons involved in adult education in group settings than there are people involved in all of elementary, secondary and higher education combined!

further study references: 130, 132, 167, 330

4. Participants in adult education are more likely to be younger than non-participants, better educated, more likely to hold a white-collar than a blue-collar job, and more likely to have family income above the average.

5. For persons of low educational attainment, the motivational factors associated with participation in adult education are primarily economically based, whereas for people of high educational attainment, the motivational factors are more often oriented towards self-actualization.

6. Participation in institutional programs of adult education is positively associated with participation in other formal organizations and voluntary associations.

> *"Each path is only one of a million paths. Therefore, you must always keep in mind that a path is only a path. If you feel that you must now follow it, you need not stay with it under any circumstances. Any path is only a path. There is no affront to yourself or others in dropping it if that is what your heart tells you to do."*
> —*Carlos Castaneda*

Adult Learners Learning on Their Own

1. Much, perhaps most, of adult learning does not take place in learning groups, but as *individual learning projects (Allen Tough)*

    -   Tough defined a "project" as a series of related learning episodes, adding up to at least seven hours, and found that "in each episode more than half of the person's total motivation is to gain and retain certain fairly clear knowledge and skill, or to produce some other lasting change in himself."

    -   It is common for a man or woman to spend 700 hours a year at learning projects.

    -   About 70% of all learning projects are planned by the learner himself who seeks help and subject matter from a variety of acquaintances, experts, and printed resources.

2. Factors positively associated with how much time an adult devotes to learning *(Allen Tough)*

    -   The extent to which the person's parents read or learned.

    -   The amount of activity or achievement in his childhood home.

    -   The use of vocabulary in his childhood home.

    -   The number of years spent in school.

    -   The characteristics and curriculum of schools attended.

    -   His satisfactions with his previous attempts to learn.

    -   His original position among his siblings (first children tend to devote more time to learning).

The Process of Learning or Change

1. Learning may be psychomotor, cognitive or affective.

   - *Psychomotor Learning* — new skills, behavior patterns, new ways of acting and doing.

   - *Cognitive Learning* — new knowledge, understanding, awareness, beliefs, new ways of thinking.

   - *Affective Learning* — new attitudes, values, priorities, new ways of feeling.

2. The process by which learning or change takes place:

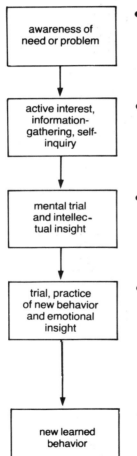

- You as learner are aware of a need or problem calling for a different way of thinking, feeling, acting.

- You may be interested enough to find out more by setting up a self-inquiry (perhaps reading about, going to a class, talking with someone). You gather information, explore alternatives, seek to understand and clarify the new way.

- You mentally practice the new behavior (have trial runs in your imagination) considering and weighing advantages and disadvantages, possible consequences, believed strength in your ability to change, etc., and thus gain "intellectual insight."

- You decide to actually practice the new behavior, try it out in a "real" situation, but you face a period of mental turmoil during the trial. In the transition, though practicing "right" you feel "wrong." With continued practice, your *intellectual* insight eventually is followed by *emotional* insight and right *feels* right.

- With emotional insight and consistent practice, the new behavior becomes "learned" and integrated — now more or less a permanent part of your way of thinking, feeling, acting.

> *"Only that day dawns to which we are awake."*
> —Henry David Thoreau

further study references: 49, 117, 161, 176, 233

APPLICATION WORKSHEET

My Adult Learning

"An Introduction to Helping Adults Learn and Change" by Russell D. Robinson, PhD

List all adult learning experiences in which you have been involved in the last three years.

GROUP EXPERIENCES (Classes, workshops, etc.)	What about the experience was most helpful for your learning?	What about the experience was least helpful for your learning?

INDIVIDUAL EXPERIENCES (Self-study projects)	What did you do that was most helpful in learning?	What did you do that was least helpful in learning?

"A man's life may stagnate as literally as water may stagnate, and just as motion and direction are the remedy for one, so purpose and activity are the remedy for the other."

—John Burroughs

"We are all functioning at a small fraction of our capacity to live fully in its total meaning of loving, caring, creating and adventuring. Consequently, the actualizing of our potential can become the most exciting adventure of our lifetime."

—Herbert Otto

"The old dog can learn new tricks but the answer is not a direct and simple one. It appears that the old dog is reluctant to learn new tricks. He is less likely to gamble on the results, particularly when he is not convinced that the new trick is any better than the old tricks, which served him so well in the past. He may not learn the new trick as rapidly as he did in the past, but learn it he does. Further, the best evidence seems to indicate that if he starts out as a clever young pup, he is very likely to end up as a wise old hound."

—Ledford J. Bischof

2 ADULT MOTIVATION
needs, perceptions, affect

> "No great improvements in the lot of mankind are possible, until a great change takes place in the fundamental institution of their modes of thought."
> —John Stewart Mill

Motivation and Learning

1. Motivation is a concept (or cluster of concepts) that attempts to explain why people behave as they do. Understanding why people behave as they do is vitally important to helping adults learn.

2. Understanding behavior involves consideration of needs (wants, desires), perceptions (assumptions, beliefs about reality), self-concept (self-esteem, self-worth), self efficacy (power), affect (feelings, fears, doubts), locus of control, cultural and social views, attitudes, and other psychosocial factors.

3. Behavior involves perceptions of expectancy, effort, likelihood of successful performance, reward, and needs satisfied.

4. Learning involves will and skill. Wanting to learn and knowing how to learn.

Theories of Learning

1. **Humanist Learning Theories** (*Rogers, Maslow, Knowles*)

    *   Focus on human potential for growth, human nature, affect (feelings).
    *   Locus of control is in the individual's inherent desire and capacity to grow, choose, learn, "become", self-actualize, take responsibility for learning.
    *   Emphasis on student-centered learning, self-initiation, self-direction, personal involvement, self-evaluation.
    *   Learning involves "unleashing motivation" that is already there to accomplish goals that satisfy needs.

2. **Cognitive Learning Theories [Gestalt]** (*Wertheimer, Kohler, Gagne, Koffka, Lewin, Piaget, Ausubel, Bruner*)

- Focus on perception, insight, meaning.
- Locus of control is in internal mental processes by which individuals process information in order to make sense, discover meaning.
- Emphasis on how information is processed, stored, and retrieved; on learning how to learn, learner's needs, learning styles, organizing activity for learning, concept learning, problem-solving.
- Learning involves sensory input and thinking (metacognition), paying attention, perception (providing meaning and significance), short term memory (working memory) and long term memory (everything that ever happened which is recoverable if you replicate the setting in which it was learned).

3. **Behaviorist Learning Theories** (*Pavlov, Watson, Thorndike, Hull, Skinner, Tolman, Guthrie*)

- Focus on observable changes of behavior.
- Locus of control is determined by elements in the environment, stimulus-response.
- Emphasis on reinforcement, connection of events, repetition.
- Learning involves controlling environment to obtain desired response.

4. **Social Learning Theories** (*Bandura, Rotter*)

- Focus on learning from the observation of other people in a social setting.
- Locus of control is in interaction of the person, the environment, and the behavior, ascribed to both external and internal causes.
- Emphasis on environment and social interactions with other people, importance of context, socialization, guiding, mentoring.
- Learning involves modeling and interactions with other people in a social context.
  (summarized from *S. Merriam* and *R. Caffarella*)

> *"In what areas do most people appear to find life's meaning? We have only one pragmatic guide: meaning must reside in the things for which people strive, the goals which they set for themselves, their wants, needs, desires and wishes."*
> — *Eduard Lindeman*

further study references: 6, 58, 74, 183, 229, 233, 266, 33

Needs

1. An individual's behavior is influenced by his/her needs, which vary from person to person and from time to time.

2. These needs are shown in a hierarchical arrangement (*Abraham Maslow*) to indicate that a need at one level tends to operate as a primary source of motivation when needs at a lower level are sufficiently satisfied for that person.

    *   *Physiological Needs* — most basic needs, important to sustain life itself, such as food, activity, air and sleep.

    *   *Security Needs* — a projection of physiological needs into the future including protection from physical harm, assurance of continuing income and employment, etc.

    *   *Social Needs* — include a sense of belonging and membership in a group and acceptance by other people.

    *   *Self-esteem Needs* — include that which reflects on an individual's self-worth and self-confidence.

    *   *Self-actualization* — refers to a sense of accomplishment and the development and utilization of one's potential capacities.

> "A mind is not to be changed by place or time, the mind is its own place, and in itself can make a Heaven of Hell, a Hell of Heaven."
> —John Milton

> "What lies behind us and what lies before us are tiny matters compared to what lies within us."
> —William Morrow

Perceptions and Assumptions

1. People behave in ways that make sense to them. They "make sense" on the basis of perceptions they hold of themselves (self-concept) and perceptions (assumptions) they hold of the situation and other persons in it.

2. It matters not whether those assumptions are true, half-true, or patently false, we behave as it they were true. Call it myth, belief or attitude, these mental sets color our thinking and our acting and thus our learning.

3. Beliefs of competence beget more competence. Likewise beliefs of failure beget failure.

4. This "assumptive world" may be narrow and localite, or cosmopolite in outlook; the more cosmopolite the world view, the more one's assumptions are open to change and re-evaluation.

5. Prejudice — pre-judgments — may be rooted simply in unquestioned assumptions picked up in childhood, or may be deep-seated assumptions of others' inferiority, adopted to prop up one's own low self-esteem.

Self-Concept

1. Self-concept is learned, largely from our interpretations of how others treat us. Once evolved, self-concept tends to be self-perpetuating, guiding our interpretations of new experiences and information and our reactions to and interactions with others.

2. People with healthy self-concepts, with high self-esteem

    • see themselves in essentially positive ways (on the whole as OK)

    • see themselves accurately and realistically (without delusions of grandeur or self-abasement)

    • are capable of accepting themselves and others (I'm OK and you're OK)

    • have a high degree of identification with other people (are able to put themselves in another's shoes, have empathy.)

3. Adults tend to see themselves as autonomous, self-directing, self-responsible, independent personalities. Adults have a deep psychological need to be treated with respect, to be perceived as having the ability to run their own lives. Adults tend to avoid, resist, and resent being placed in situations in which they feel they are treated like children — told what to do and what not to do, talked down to, embarrassed, punished, judged.

4. Adults who believe that what *they* do makes a difference in their lives, who have a sense of power over their experience, are motivated to learn. In contrast, adults who feel powerless, alienated, who feel that what they do cannot change fate or the system, are motivated *not* to learn.

             further study references: 80, 116, 158, 223, 249, 257, 274, 277, 297

Motivating Learners

1. The Impostor Syndrome *(Stephen Brookfield)*

   - Learners sometimes see themselves as "impostors" accompanied by a feeling of not belonging when they see how capable and confident other students are and compare that with what they see as their own poor abilities and doubts. Not uncommon for learners in new situations.

   - To help a learner with "impostor syndrome"

     1) Regularly affirm the student's sense of self-worth.
     2) Acknowledge that you have felt the same way sometimes as learner and/or teacher.
     3) Encourage students to communicate their feelings with each other so they know they are not the only ones who may feel this way.

2. How Teachers Enhance Learner Motivation *(Raymond Wlodkowski)*

   - At the beginning of the learning experience: when the learner enters and starts the learning process, the motivating teacher addresses these issues:

     1) Attitudes. What can I do to establish a positive learner attitude toward this learning experience?
     2) Needs. How do I best meet the needs of the learners in this learning experience?

   - During the learning experience: when the learner is involved in the main content of the learning process, the motivating teacher addresses these issues:

     1) Stimulation. What about this learning experience will continuously stimulate the learners.
     2) Affect. How is the affective or emotional climate for this learning experience a positive one for learners?

   - At the end of the learning experience: when the learner is completing or ending the learning process, the motivating teacher addresses these issues:

     1) Competence. How does this learning experience increase or affirm learner feelings of competence?
     2) Reinforcement. What is the reinforcement that this learning experience provides for the learners?

Emotions

1. Taking Charge of Your Feelings *(Wayne Dyer)*

   - Recognize that we choose how we feel.

     Examples:
     1) Don't say, "You hurt my feelings,"
        but say, "I hurt my feelings because of things I told myself about your reactions to me."
     2) Don't say, "You made me feel bad,"
        but say, "I made myself feel bad."
     3) Don't say, "He makes me sick,"
        but say, "I make myself sick."
     4) Don't say, "You made a fool of me in public,"
        but say, "I made myself feel foolish by taking your opinions of me more seriously than my own, and believing that others would do the same."
     5) Don't say, "I can't help the way I feel,"
        but say, "I can help the way I feel and I have chosen to be upset."

   - Your Erroneous Zones (9 ways guaranteed to make yourself feel miserable).

     1) Approval Seeking

        —Obsessive concern about what others think

        —Belief that disapproval of you belongs to the other, not you

        Challenge: Break the chain between what others think, say or do, and your own self-worth.

     2) Living in the Past

        —Accepting the self-labels "That's me," "I've always been that way," "I can't help it," etc.

        —If you live in the past you will be doomed to repeat it over and over again.

        Challenge: Give up self-imposed limits of the past

     3) Guilt and Worry

        —Guilt about the past; worry about the future. But guilt doesn't change the past and worry doesn't change the future.

        Challenge: Learn to live in the *now.*

     4) Fear of Unknown

        —Another name for resistance to change, resistance to anything new; what we fear, we avoid

        —Not trying because you may not do it well is the excuse of the perfectionist.

        Challenge: Try something new.

> *"I will act as if what I do makes a difference."*
> — *William James*

further study references: 21, 68, 116, 143, 246

5) The Tyranny of the "Shoulds"

—Putting your shoulds on other people and becoming disappointed or angry when people don't do what they "should" do.

—Worshipping those who live up to your shoulds and blaming those who don't.

—Playing the F.O.O.L.(Focusing On Other's Lives)

Challenge: Accept others as they are.

6) Demand for Justice

—Notion that everything has to be fair.

—Jealousy is a "demand for Justice" sideshow.

Challenge: Recognize that absolute justice is not possible in human affairs.

7) Procrastination

—"Putting it off" avoids today, avoids doing anything now.

—Accompanied by inertia of hoping, wishing and maybe.

—The habit of procrastination produces critics rather than doers.

—A spinoff of Procrastination is Boredom, the result of a choice to put off doing anything.

Challenge: Do it now!

8) Dependency

—Not wanting to "leave the nest" and become one's own person.

—Accompanied by fear of independence and autonomy.

—Dependency is a choice: You are treated the way you teach others to treat you.

Challenge: Maintain your autonomy.

9) Anger

—Antidote to anger is to eliminate the internal sentence, "If only you were more like me (. . .then I wouldn't be so angry!)."

—Anger is debilitating, dis-ease producing.

—Like all emotions, anger is the result of thinking; you can choose to laugh as easily as to be angry.

Challenge: Choose not anger.

> *"If an individual is able to love productively, he loves himself too; if he can love only others, he cannot love at all."*
>
> —*Erich Fromm*

> *"We have committed the Golden Rule to memory; let us now commit it to life."*
>
> —*Edwin Markham*

2. Your Thinking and Your Emotions *(Maxie Maultsby)*

- You can change the way you *feel* by changing the way you *think*.

- The ABC's of how emotions are made:
  - (A) Your perceptions (what you see, hear, physically feel, etc.)
  - (B) Your evaluative thoughts (the thoughts you believe to be true).
  - (C) Your emotional feelings, which may be
    —relatively positive
    —relatively negative
    —relatively neutral
    —some mixture of the three

- Shortcut to emotions ("a programmed response")
  - (A) Specific perception (see snake).
    Skip *thinking,* and immediately substitute attitude or *belief* (snakes are poisonous)
  - (C) Habitual feeling (fear)

- Rules for Rational Behavior: Behavior is rational if—
  1) it's based on objective reality or the known relevant facts of a life situation.
  2) it enables you to protect your life
  3) it enables you to achieve your goals more quickly
  4) it enables you to keep out of significant trouble with other people
  5) it enables you to prevent or quickly eliminate personal emotional conflict

- Emotions can be changed by applying the rules of rational behavior (above) to the *second stage of evaluative thinking* (examining your beliefs). This process Maultsby calls "self-talk," a rational debate with yourself, using the rules of rational thinking and a decision to *change your thinking* (beliefs) which will result in a change in your emotional response.

- This process is helped by mental rehearsal or mental practice of the desired response which Maultsby calls "rational emotive imagery."

- The process of giving up an incorrect belief:
  1) Make a sincere announcement that you've given up the old belief.
  2) Recognize you still have the old belief but refuse to use the old belief anymore to explain your present experience.
  3) Explain your old and present life experience using your *new* belief.
  4) Continue to think in terms of the new belief, while acting "as if" you believe it (habitually practice believing the new belief).

> *"It is not the facts and events that upset man, but the view he takes of them."*
> —*Epictetus*

further study references: 69, 216, 222

The Self-creation Principle

1. Every behavior or act results in strengthening the motive or attitude behind the act. Every time you do something, the motivating idea or feeling that prompted you to do it is intensified *(George Weinberg)*

    - Act out of an attitude of suspicion and you will become more suspicious (*not* finding evidence you're looking for makes you *more* suspicious).

    - Act out of an attitude of fear and whatever you do will make you more afraid.

    - Act out of anger and every act will make you become more angry (the more you act out the anger, the angrier you become).

    - Act out of an attitude of resentment and you will become more resentful.

    - Act out of an attitude of confidence and you will become more confident with each act.

    - Act out of an attitude of love and you will strengthen your love (love is strengthened by doing loving acts, by *giving* love, not by receiving it; that is why, when you do something to please another regardless of what the other is doing, you will feel good, but if done *in order to* get a response, you will end up not liking the other or yourself!).

2. Every personal feeling or belief, every attitude towards ourselves, towards others, towards the threats and promises of the world, is put there by *us*. What we are responsive to is not relationships in the past but *actions* in the present. All personal feelings and beliefs can be traced to current actions that sustain them. *Not* acting on an attitude extinguishes it.

3. Positively or negatively, any act strengthens the motive or attitude behind the act. The key to the usefulness of the principle of self-creation lies in this: Your thought commands your actions; you can choose to change your actions. Choosing to change an action, and then acting on the choice, will strengthen the motivation for the choice and it will be easier to act the next time. The sheer act of acting on any belief or feeling makes you believe or feel it more.

4. The secret to controlling our own lives lies in precisely this: *acting* on only those ideas and feelings that we want to live with. Persons who want to live in fear, tensions, greed, have the formula they need; so do those who choose love, trust, confidence and zest.

> "*Every man is his own Pygmalion, and spends his life fashioning himself.*"
>
> —*I. F. Stone*

Planning for Self-change

1. Start with an examination of your present behavior *(William Glasser)*

   - Is it helping or not? (Is it helping you or someone else?)

   - Don't talk about your feelings, instead talk about *specific things you are doing* (remember, when you change what you are doing, your feelings will change too).

   - Don't ask, Why? (even if you could find out *why,* you'd still only know *why!)*

   - Deal with *present behavior* only, not past. Ask, What am I doing now? What am I thinking now? Is it helping?

2. Select a small area to change. Begin with small steps.

   - Be positive! *What will you do* (not negative: what won't you do any more)

   - Set realistic achievable goals (don't program yourself for failure).

   - State *specifically* what behavior it is you're going to do (not vague "I'm going to be nice.")

3. Establish a repetitive plan of action.

   - Make a *plan* to change a behavior, a plan of action that is specific, realistic, positive, and can be done regularly.

   - Do not make your plan contingent on what another will do or not do.

4. Do it.

   - Don't give up.

   - Don't permit yourself excuses.

> *"A man can do what he ought to do; and when he says he cannot, it is because he will not."*
> — *James Anthony Froude*

> *"Finish each day and be done with it. You have done what you could. Some blunders and absurdities no doubt crept in; forget them as soon as you can. Tomorrow is a new day; begin it well and serenely, and with too high a spirit to be cumbered with your old nonsense. This day is all that is good and fair. It is too dear with its hopes and invitations to waste a moment on the yesterdays."*
> —*Ralph Waldo Emerson*

APPLICATION WORKSHEET

Myself and Others

"An Introduction to Helping Adults Learn and Change" by Russell D. Robinson, PhD

COMPLETE THESE SENTENCES:

1. I really get into learning something when _____

_____

_____

2. Change is difficult for me when _____

_____

_____

3. When someone feels inadequate, I _____

_____

_____

4. People will take responsibility when _____

_____

_____

5. I don't like it when people trust me _____

_____

_____

6. I trust those who _____

_____

_____

7. My greatest strength is _____

_____

_____

8. Those who really know me think I am _____

_____

_____

"*One can look at psychologists as being seated under the same circus tent in which the child psychologist is sitting—the child psychologist sits. . .too near the entrance while the gerontologist sits too near the exit. Both groups really have been missing the main show—that is, what's going on in the three-ring circus that we call adulthood.*"

—*Bernice L. Neugarten*

"*We are not unlike a particularly hardy crustacean. The lobster grows by developing and shedding a series of hard, protective shells. Each time it expands from within, the confining shell must be sloughed off. It is left exposed and vulnerable until, in time, a new covering grows to replace the old. With each passage. . .we, too, must shed a protective structure. We are left exposed and vulnerable—but also yeasty and embryonic again, capable of stretching in ways we hadn't known before.*"

—*Gail Sheehy*

"*Like a butterfly, an adult is supposed to emerge fully formed and on cue after a succession of developmental stages in childhood. . .Equipped with. . .wisdom and rationality, the adult supposedly remains quiescent for another half century or so. While children change, adults only age!*"

—*Roger Gould*

3 ADULT DEVELOPMENT
transitions and learning

> "We can't always control what happens to us. We can control what we think about what happens. . .and what we are thinking is our 'life' at any particular moment."
> —Norman G. Shidle

Adult Life Cycle

1. The works of Gould, Levinson, Vaillant, Erikson, Neugarten, Gilligan, Lowenthal and others, and the enormous popularity of Sheehy's *Passages* point to a growing body of theory on adult development which is already having an impact similar to the impact on public thought of the earlier work on "stages" of childhood and adolescence.

2. Adult Life Cycle Assumptions *(Vivian Rogers McCoy)*

    *   Life unfolds in sequence and in stages.

    *   Each stage is marked by a crisis, a turning point, a crucial period of both vulnerability and potential.

    *   At transition points, progress or falling back occurs, but whichever happens, the future is substantially different.

    *   Each period has specific tasks to be engaged in; when these are successfully engaged, we move on.

    *   External (to us) marker events are constantly happening — graduations, marriage, childbirth, divorce, jobs. Changes within those marker events are what make up a developmental stage.

    *   An adult's life involves both (a) membership in the culture — jobs, class, family, society — and (b) how his/her values, aspirations, goals are being met or frustrated by participation in the world.

    *   It is in the inner realm where crucial shifts of growth occur. How we feel about the marker events, especially "off-timing" or unanticipated life events, determines if we move on or stagnate.

    *   Transitions, passages, are predictable and growth-producing.

    *   Engaging change is scary, unsettling. Regression, accommodation, and integration of change usually characterize passage.

    *   For growth to occur, challenges need to be slightly greater than the individual's present coping skills so that he/she can stretch, yet not be overwhelmed and forced to retreat to safer ground.

3. As with the conceptions of child development, the conception of ages and stages of adults is only "true" for one-third of all adults at a particular age; another one-third are ahead and one-third behind. But the sequence tends to occur on schedule.

Transitions

1. The more difficult transitions for most people appear to be (give or take two or three years):
   - age 30 — when youthful dreams have had to come to grips with reality (sometimes more difficult for women)
   - age 40 — when each comes face to face with the fact that half of one's life is over (sometimes more difficult for men);
   - age 50 — concerns about life purpose (sometimes more difficult for women);
   - age 60 — facing retirement (sometimes more difficult for men);

2. Particular problems between spouses may be engendered at transition points when one is "out of sync" with the other's stage or crisis and misinterpreting the other's "strange" behavior.

3. Early work was based primarily on studies of men. Subsequent studies of women indicate more diverse and non-linear patterns of development, the centrality of relationships throughout women's lives, and the continued importance of issues of identity and intimacy.

Early Adulthood

1. In early adulthood, according to Erikson, the issue is intimacy (relating to other people) vs. isolation.

2. *Ages 18—22 — Pulling Up Roots (Sheehy, Gould, Levinson and others)*

   - The transition from adolescence to adulthood; leaving the family establishing life on one's own, defining identity.

   - Continuing educational preparation, beginning work, handling peer relationships, establishing a separate "home," managing time and money.

3. *Ages 22—28 – Becoming Adult (Sheehy, Levinson, Gould and others)*

   - Reaching out; trying out the "dream;" establishing autonomy.

   - Setting in motion life patterns; selecting a mate; beginning career ladder, establishing a family, becoming a parent.

   - Finding a mentor, someone about 15 years older.

   - Often characterized by doing what we feel we should.

   - Characterized by feeling that we are different, special, that we can do anything.

4. *Ages 28—33 — Catch-30 (Sheehy, Levinson, Gould and others)*

   - The age 30 transition characterized by second thoughts, a feeling of being too narrow and restricted with earlier choices of career, marriage, relationships. Identity concerns, especially for women.

   - Characterized by a new vitality, and is often a time of change, turmoil and dissatisfaction.

   - Urges to broaden oneself, make new choices, alter or deepen commitments, change jobs, buy a house, have a baby, get a divorce, etc. Family-career conflicts for women.

- Urge to do what one wants to do rather than follow the earlier "shoulds."

- Time of reappraisal, putting down roots, searching for personal values.

Middle Adulthood

1. In middle adulthood, according to Erikson, the issue is generativity (a commitment to and caring for next generation) vs. stagnation.

2. Middle Age (35 – 60) is generally the most powerful stage in life in terms of earning capacity, influence on other people and impact on society in general. Middle age is the age of society's norm-bearers and decision-makers, bill-payers and power-brokers, managers, and leaders — society's movers and shakers.

3. *Ages 33—38 — Becoming One's Own Person (Levinson, Gould, Sheehy and others)*

   - Rooting and extending, a period of reaching out.

   - Establishing one's niche in society, developing competence.

   - Working at "making it," striving to advance and progress; career consolidation. Sheey calls ages 35—45 "deadline decade."

   - Relating to one's family: spouse, children, parents.

   - Conflicting time demands.

   > "In the middle of the journey of our life I came to myself within a dark wood where the straight-way was lost. Ah, how hard a thing it is to tell of that wood, savage and harsh and dense, the thought of which renews my fear. So bitter is it that death is hardly more."
   >
   > —*Dante Alighieri at age 37*
   > *(opening of* Divine Comedy*)*

4. *Ages 38—46 — Midlife Transition (Levinson, Sheehy, Gould and others)*

   - Often an unstable, explosive time, resembling adolescence, brought on by the emotional awareness that time is running out.

   - The mentor now cast aside, the mid-lifer emerges ready to mentor a younger person.

   - Reassessment of marriage.

   - Reexamine work and career goals.

   - Relating to teen-age children and aging parents.

   - Search for meaning.

   - A reversal between men and women — women becoming more aggressive and masculine and men becoming more feminine.

     1) Women who have been homemakers are re-defining themselves (as opposed to being defined by their husbands or children), beginning careers, reaching out from the home.

25

2)   Men are often readjusting their career aspirations downward with the feeling of being trapped with dreams unrealized, turning back to the home.

- Dramatic changes may take place in an effort to bring the dream back (for men) or build a new dream (for women) and these efforts may bring to the fore formerly suppressed aspects of self.

- The mid-life crisis may increase vulnerability to extra-marital affairs, alcoholism, divorce, over-eating, or even suicide.

> *"The hormone production levels are dropping, the head is balding, the sexual vigor is diminishing, the stress is unending, the children are leaving, the parents are dying, the job horizons are narrowing . . . the past floats by in a fog of hopes not realized, opportunities not grasped . . . potentials not fulfilled, and the future is a confrontation with one's mortality."*
> —M.W. Lear, *"Is There a Male Menopause?"* in N.Y.Times, 1/28/73

5. *Ages 46—53 — Settling Down (Levinson, Sheehy, Gould and others)*

- Following the mid-life crisis, formation of a new life structure.

- Committed to new choices, the die is cast, decisions must be lived with, life settles down.

- If changed too little in the mid-life crisis, there may be a major age 50 transition, especially for women.

- Discovery we are ultimately alone and only we are responsible for our lives.

6. *Ages 53—60 — Renewal or Resignation (Sheehy, Gould, Levinson and others)*
- If one has successfully passed the midlife transition, this will be a time of renewal of purpose and revitalization, of self-acceptance, realism and warmth.

- A time of increased personal happiness and satisfaction, including one's career and marriage.

- If one has not dealt successfully with the midlife passage, this will be a period of resignation.

- Development of secondary interests in preparation for one's later years.

Later Adulthood

1. In later adulthood, according to Erikson, the issue is integrity (a belief that one's life has had a purpose) vs. despair.

2. *Ages 60—65 — Late Adult Transition (Levinson, Gould and others)*

- This transition brings retirement or anticipation (or dread) of retirement.

- It may be especially difficult for those who have largely defined themselves by their careers. Women who have not worked, often make this transition more easily than either men or women who have previously had their time structured and energies absorbed by careers.

- Adjustments to less income.

- Confronted by loss (loss of job, loss of home, loss of spouse), the older adult may react with alienation, a sense of powerlessness, meaninglessness, isolation, self-estrangement, futility or despair. Or the older adult may choose to meet the crisis as a challenge to be mastered, and continue to grow.

- Expand avocational interests, do those things "I've always wanted to do."

3. *Ages 65 and up — Late Adulthood (Neugarten, Levinson and others)*

- With advancing age, engagement, rather than disengagement, is more closely associated with psychological well-being.

- Older persons who are educationally active tend to have greater zest for living, a better self-concept, and are more generally satisfied with their lives.

- Although religious practices (like attending church) tend to decrease in later years, religious feelings and beliefs increase.

- Phases of Retirement *(R. T. Atchley)*
  1) Preretirement (anticipation)
  2) Honeymoon (euphoria at newfound freedom)
  3) Disenchantment (missing the former life)
  4) Reorientation (finding new interests)
  5) Stability (routinization)

- Retirement Career Profile of Choices *(Doris and Burton Kreitlow)*

  1) Regressive Choice: the disengaged
  2) Neutral Choices: the self-centered, the house sitter, the club or center sitter
  3) Growth Choices: the new producer (new career), the contributor (volunteer), the pursuer of a cause
  4) Soaring Choice: the self-actualized

- Five Periods of Older Adulthood *(James C. Fisher)*

  1) Continuity with Middle Age (retirement plans pursued, middle age lifestyle continued, other activities substituted for work)
  2) Early Transition (involuntary or voluntary transitional events such as death of spouse, relocation, resulting end of continuity with middle age)
  3) Revised Lifestyle (adaptation to changes, stable lifestyle appropriate to older adulthood, socialization through age-group affiliation)
  4) Later Transition (loss of autonomy, health, mobility; need for assistance and/or care)
  5) Final Period (adaptation to changes, stable lifestyle appropriate to level of dependency, sense of finitude, mortality)

APPLICATION WORKSHEET

My Adult Life

"An Introduction to Helping Adults Learn and Change" by Russell D. Robinson, PhD

Age	Characteristics	Write below your own career events, family events, important life experiences
18—22	Pulling up roots; leaving the family; establishing life on one's own.	
22—28	Reaching out; trying out the "vision;" establishing autonomy; setting in motion life patterns; finding a mentor; entering world of adult work; confidence; optimism.	
28—33	Age 30 transition; "Catch 30;" questioning of earlier choices; doubts, the urge to change, to broaden and extend oneself; desire for stability and roots.	
33—38	Rooting and extending; becoming one's own person.	
38—46	Midlife transition; feeling time is running out; dissatisfaction; re-examination; urgency; "deadline decade."	
46—53	Restabilization; settling down; self-assessment; feeling "die is cast;" mellowing; self-acceptance.	
53—60	Renewal or resignation; maintaining position or changing roles.	
60—65	Late Adulthood transition; retirement; preparation for later years.	
65—	Late Adulthood; feelings of fulfillment or failure; search for meaning of one's life.	

Aging

1. Adults can learn throughout the life span. The capacity to learn does not diminish with age, only the rate or speed of learning and even this rate of decline is primarily in adults who are out of the practice of learning. Learning is the best cure for an adult's inability to learn!

2. Differences in adult learning ability relate more to such factors as social status, educational background, occupational level, and native intelligence, than to age differences.

3. Certain physiological changes take place during adult years (but with wide individual variations):

   - Some decline in visual acuity;

   - Some decline in audio acuity;

   - Some slowing up of physical tempo and decline in energy;

   - Some lowering of tolerance for cold, heat, fatigue;

   - Such physiological changes often create a need for defenses against the losses. Defenses may be manifested as
     1) limiting choices
     2) intolerance for ambiguity
     3) assuming extreme positions without apparent justification

4. Though muscular strength, vigor and speed of reaction tend to decline, *skills* tend to increase with long practice.

5. Though exhibiting less intense drive or ambition, there may be increasing reliability, calmness and serenity and a greater concern for accuracy over volume.

6. The greatest barrier to learning for older adults is their belief that "you can't teach an old dog new tricks," and previous negative learning experiences.

7. In any case, one's attitude toward age is more important than age itself, as a determiner of experience.

"Worry kills man, fear kills man, hate kills man, jealousy kills man. Man doesn't do these things with his intellect; he worries, fears, hates and is jealous with his organs. Man is a mechanism run by electricity, a machine made up of twenty-eight trillion electrical cells. Electricity keeps the flame of life burning in the cell. In a hate jag or a fear or jealousy drunk you destroy an irreplaceable part of yourself."
—*George Crile, M.D.*

"The afternoon of life must also have a significance of its own and cannot be merely a pitiful appendage to life's morning."
— *Carl Jung*

---

further study references: 23, 24, 49, 120, 136, 138, 162, 182, 205, 285

Intelligence

1. Two Kinds of Intelligence (*R. B. Cattell*)

   - Fluid intelligence--considered to be "innate" intelligence, usually associated with timed tests (like IQ), generally thought to decline with aging.

   - Crystallized intelligence--considered to be influenced more by education and experience, which tends to increase with aging.

2. Theory of Multiple Intelligences (*Howard Gardner*)

   - Howard Gardner in *Frames of Mind* identifies seven discrete intelligences in contrast to the conventional narrower view of intelligence as measured by IQ and similar tests.

     1) Linguistic—Sensitivity to the meaning and order of words (poet, translator)
     2) Logical-Mathematical—Ability to handle chains of reasoning and to recognize patterns and order (mathematician, scientist)
     3) Musical—Sensitivity to pitch, melody, rhythm and tone (composer, singer)
     4) Bodily-Kinesthetic—Ability to use the body skillfully and handle objects adroitly (athlete, dancer)
     5) Spacial—Ability to perceive the world accurately and to re-create or transform aspects of that world (sculptor, architect, surveyor)
     6) Interpersonal—Ability to understand people and relationships (politician, salesman)
     7) Intrapersonal—Access to one's emotional life as a means to understand oneself and others (therapist, social worker)

"I call systems thinking the fifth discipline because it is the conceptual cornerstone that underlies all of the five learning disciplines [personal mastery, mental models, building shared vision, team learning] . . . All are concerned with a shift of mind from seeing parts to seeing wholes, from seeing people as helpless reactors to seeing them as active participants in shaping their reality, from reacting to the present to creating the future."

— Peter M. Senge

further study references: 73, 87, 206, 228

Moral Development

1. Stages of Moral Development (*Lawrence Kohlberg*)

   - Punishment and obedience orientation (avoid punishment and defer to power)

   - Instrumental relativist orientation (satisfy one's own needs primarily with reciprocal "you scratch my back and I'll scratch yours")

   - Interpersonal concord orientation (win approval by pleasing and helping others by "being nice")

   - Law and order orientation (follow authority, obey fixed rules and maintain social order; do one's duty)

   - Social contract legalistic orientation (agree on general individual rights and standards with possibility of changing law in accord with changing personal values and opinion)

   - Universal ethical principle orientation (choose ethical principles which are logically comprehensive, universal and consistent, such as justice, equality, dignity of the individual)

> *"The voluntary path to cheerfulness, if our spontaneous cheerfulness be lost, is to sit up cheerfully, and act and speak as if cheerfulness were already there. To feel brave, act as if we were brave, use all our will to that end, and courage will very likely replace fear. If we act as if from some better feeling, the bad feeling soon folds its tent like an Arab and silently steals away."*
> —William James

Human Response to Change

1. Phases in responding to personal life change (*Gordon Lippitt*)

   - Shock
   - Disbelief *(It can't be happening)*
   - Guilt *(What did I do to cause this?)*
   - Projection *(blaming, anger, rage)*
   - Rationalization *(finding reasons to justify)*
   - Integration *(how change can fit into life)*
   - Acceptance of change

2. Stress of adjusting to change *(Thomas H. Holmes)*

- Events of life have been found to produce individual stress reactions. Life Change Units have been scaled for each event to reflect the relative amount of stress and disruption typically associated with each event.

- Life changes, whether sudden or predictable, situational or developmental, for better or for worse, have an effect on all of us. The effect is "stress."

- The "stress response" (readiness for "fight or flight") has been part of man's physiological make-up from the beginning, providing preparedness in dangerous or challenging situations. The involuntary responses that make up the stress syndrome include: increased blood pressure, increased heart rate, increased rate of respiration (breathing), increased flow of blood to the muscles, and increased metabolism.

- As the total number of scale values accumulated in a 12-month period increases, connection between life crises and illness becomes more evident. When life crises in one year scored a total between 150 and 199 life-change units, only 37 percent of persons had associated health changes (an illness occurring within two years of the life crises). When a moderate number of life crises occurred (scores between 200 and 299 life-change units), 51 percent were accompanied by health changes. For people having major life crises (300 or more life-change units) health changes occurred within one to two years for 79 percent of the individuals.

3. There are things people can do to cope with change and the impact of stress and the demands for adaptation.

- Consciously make an effort to reduce the general levels of sensory stimulation for short periods of time (get away from it all).

- Maintain "stability zones" in the presence of change (keeping old and familiar things, old friends, long term relationships).

- Anticipate a change and consciously and carefully plan for it (get used to the idea, learn more about it).

- Join temporary "situational groups" (support groups) with other people going through the same transition or change at the same time (share common adaptive experiences and support each other).

- Link with someone for person to person crisis counseling (someone to talk to).

- Recognize that circumstances and events do not of themselves produce stress, but our attitudes and perceptions about the event. Consciously examine and change those attitudes, beliefs and perceptions.

- Learn to relax. Practice a "relaxation response" (letting go) when you feel yourself beginning to tighten up.

APPLICATION WORKSHEET

My Life Event Changes

"An Introduction to Helping Adults Learn and Change" by Russell D. Robinson, PhD

SCORE YOURSELF FOR A 12-MONTH PERIOD

Life Events	Life Change Units	My Score
Death of Spouse	100	
Divorce	73	
Marital separation from mate	65	
Detention in jail or other institution	63	
Death of a close family member	63	
Major personal injury or illness	53	
Marriage	50	
Being fired at work	47	
Marital reconciliation with mate	45	
Retirement from work	45	
Major change in health or behavior of family member	44	
Pregnancy	40	
Sexual difficulties	39	
Gain of new family member (birth, adoption, oldster moving in)	39	
Major business readjustment (merger, reorganization)	39	
Change in financial state (lot worse off, or lot better off)	38	
Death of close friend	37	
Change to different line of work	36	
Increased arguing with spouse	35	
Taking on mortgage over $10,000 (purchasing home, business)	31	
Foreclosure of mortgage or loan	30	
Change in responsibilities at work (promotion, demotion, transfer)	29	
Son or daughter leaving home	29	
Trouble with in-laws	29	
Outstanding personal achievement	28	
Spouse begins or stops work	26	
Begin or end formal schooling	26	
Change in living conditions (new home, remodeling)	25	
Revision of personal habits (dress, manners, associations)	24	
Trouble with boss	23	
Major change in work hours or conditions	20	
Change in residence	20	
Change in schools	20	
Major change in usual type or amount of recreation	19	
Change in church activities (a lot more, a lot less)	19	
Change in social activities (clubs, dancing, movies, visiting)	18	
Taking on mortgage or loan less than $10,000 (car, TV, freezer)	17	
Change in sleeping habits (when or amount)	16	
Change in family reunions/get-togethers (lot more or less)	15	
Change in eating habits (lot more or less, different time or place)	15	
Vacation	13	
Christmas	12	
Minor violations of the law (traffic tickets, warnings)	11	

> *"Change — real change — comes from the inside out. It doesn't come from hacking at the leaves of attitude and behavior with quick fix personality ethic techniques. It comes from striking at the root — the fabric of our thought, the fundamental, essential paradigms, which give definition to our character and create the lens through which we see the world."*
>
> *— Stephen R. Covey*

> *"The transition from a paradigm in crisis to a new one from which a new tradition of normal science can emerge is far from a cumulative process, one achieved by an articulation or extension of the old paradigm. Rather it is a reconstruction of the field from new fundamentals, a reconstruction that changes some of the field's most elementary theoretical generalizations as well as many of its paradigm methods and applications."*
>
> *— Thomas S. Kuhn*

> *"Be not conformed to this world; but be ye transformed by the renewing of your mind."*
>
> *— St. Paul*

4 ADULT CHANGE
transformational learning

> *"Why are mental models so powerful in affecting what we do? In part, because they affect what we see. As psychologists say, we observe selectively."*
> — *Peter M. Senge*

Paradigms and Mental Models

1. Learning is transformational to the extent that it requires a paradigm shift in perspective.

2. A paradigm is usually defined as an accepted model or pattern. *Thomas Kuhn* and others use the term more broadly to describe a "world view," an established way of looking at things. A paradigm shift is a shift of vision, to perceive in a new way, to see things differently. It amounts to a transformation to a different view of reality, a new mental model.

3. All people are to a greater or lesser extent "trapped" by mental models that cause them to reject new insights that conflict with deeply held internal images of how the world works, images that limit them to familiar ways of thinking and acting.

4. Transformational learning is fundamentally an intuitive and creative act of challenging heretofore taken-for-granted assumptions about reality.

5. Transformational learning involves critical reflection, questioning, exploring, examining, discovering, reframing, inventing, and thus to some degree, transforming assumptions underlying our beliefs, values, accepted truths, perceptions, behaviors, and social structures. It is, so to speak, to step into a new world.

Challenging Assumptions

1. Assumptions are rarely wholly right or wholly wrong. They may be valid in some situations and invalid or less valid in others. Recognizing the conditions and contexts that render assumptions invalid or less valid is fundamental to transformational change.

2. Assumptions are the rules of thumb that guide our actions, the common sense beliefs and conventional wisdom that have been "ratified" by our interpretations of experience.

---

3. Brookfield refers to "critical thinking" as that which "involves calling into question the assumptions underlying our customary, habitual ways of thinking and acting and then being ready to think and act differently on the basis of this critical questioning."

4. The process has also been referred to as critical analysis, critical awareness, critical consciousness, critical reflection, emancipatory learning, perspective transformation, reflective learning, etc.

5. By whatever name, critical thinking is regarded as a productive and positive activity people engage in when creating and re-creating aspects of their personal, workplace, and political lives.

6. Critical thinking is emotive as well as rational. Asking critical questions about previously accepted values, ideas, and behaviors is anxiety-producing and involves our deepest emotional responses.

7. Critical reflection values one's maintaining a thoughtful skepticism with respect to belief systems, habitual behaviors, and social structures.

8. There is an implicit assumption that adults through critical reflection will choose superior perspectives as they better understand the meaning of their experience.

9. New learning by its nature transforms existing knowledge into a new perspective and in so doing may be said to "emancipate" or empower the learner.

Models of Critical Reflection

1. Several models have been developed to describe the process of examining the assumptions underlying actions and considering new ways of looking at the world and living in it.

2. **Reflection-in-Action (*Donald Schon*)**

   - A situation brings a spontaneous, routinized "knowing-in-action" response consisting of strategies, understandings and ways of framing the task or problem which were arrived at without conscious deliberation.

   - When routine responses lead to an unexpected outcome a "surprise" occurs.

   - Surprise leads to reflection-in-action. Reflection causes one to consciously consider both the unexpected event and the knowing-in-action that led up to it.

- Reflection-in-action critically questions the assumptional structure of knowing-in-action, thinking critically of the thinking that led up to this action and possibly restructuring strategies of action, understandings of phenomena, and reframing problems.

- Reflection gives rise to on-the-spot experiment, trying out new actions, testing tentative new understandings, making moves to change. On-the-spot experiment may work, or it may produce surprises that call for further reflection and experiment.

2. Perspective Transformation (*Jack Mezirow*)

- A "disorienting dilemma" to which old patterns of response are ineffective.

- A self-examination and assessment of assumptions and beliefs.

- Revision of "specific assumptions about oneself and others until the very structure of assumptions becomes transformed."

> *"Perspective transformation is the process of becoming critically aware of how and why our presuppositions have come to constrain the way we perceive, understand, and feel about our world; of reformulating these assumptions to permit a more inclusive, discriminating, permeable, and integrative perspective; and of making decisions or otherwise acting upon these new understandings."*
> — *Jack Mezirow*

3. Conscientization (*Paulo Freire*)

- Freire defines conscientization as "the process in which men, not as recipients, but as knowing subjects, achieve a deepening awareness both of the sociocultural reality which shapes their lives and of their capacity to transform reality."

- Education, by providing an increasing awareness of one's situation, involves moving from the lowest level of consciousness, where there is no comprehension of how forces shape one's life, to the highest level of critical consciousness.

- Education involves problem posing with teachers and students as coinvestigators in dialogue seeking to humanize and liberate their common reality.

- The ultimate goal is liberation, "the action and reflection of men upon their world in order to transform it."

4. **Process of Critical Thinking** (*Stephen Brookfield*)

- **Trigger event**. An unexpected happening triggered by a positive or negative event causes us to question previously trusted assumptions.

- **Appraisal and self-scrutiny**. Alternating between minimization and denial we identify and challenge assumptions that underlie beliefs, values, and actions that we have taken for granted, and the context that supports these assumptions.

- **Exploration**. Imagining and exploring alternatives to existing ways of thinking and living we search for new ways of explaining and behaving.

- **Developing alternative perspectives**. Gaining some new insight or changed perspective, we begin learning new ways.

- **Integration**. We begin integrating new ways into our lives.

> *"Suspending assumptions . . . does not mean throwing out our assumptions, suppressing them, or avoiding their expression. Nor, in any way, does it say that having opinions is bad, or that we should eliminate subjectivism. Rather, it means being aware of our assumptions and holding them up for examination. This cannot be done if we are defending our opinions. Nor, can it be done if we are unaware of our assumptions, or unaware that our views are based on assumptions, rather than incontrovertible fact."*
>
> — *Peter M. Senge*

Facilitating Creative Thinking

1. Dialogue (*David Bohm*)

- Dialogue is different from discussion. As practiced, discussion (from the same root as percussion and concussion) is often for the purpose of having one's views prevail. In contrast dialogue (from Greek *dialogos* denotes a free flow of meaning between people).

- In dialogue, Bohm says, a group accesses a larger "pool of common meaning," which cannot be accessed individually. The purpose of dialogue is to go beyond any one individual's understanding as group participants explore their assumptions. In dialogue,

  1) all participants must suspend their assumptions,
  2) all participants must regard one another as colleagues,
  3) there must be a facilitator who keeps the dialogue on track.

further study references: 37, 289

- Dialogue maintains a spirit of inquiry enabling people to explore the thinking behind their views, their deeper assumptions and the evidence they have that leads them to these views.

2. Some teaching techniques for imagining alternatives (*Brookfield*)

   - Brainstorming (structured spontaneity)

   - Envisioning alternative futures

   - Developing preferred scenarios (detailed, concrete descriptions of desired state)

   - Future invention (process including goal formulation, indicator invention, consequence forecasting, value-shift assessment, scenario construction, writing futures histories, planning tactics, taking action)

   - Scenario analysis (use of hypothetical scenarios)

   - Simulations for decision making in a crisis

3. Characteristics of creative thinkers (*Brookfield*)

   - Reject standardized formats for problem solving

   - Have a wide range of related and divergent interests

   - Have multiple perspectives on a problem

   - View the world in relative rather than absolute terms

   - Use experimental and trial and error methods

   - Have a future orientation; embrace change

   - Have self-confidence and trust own judgment

> "Two groups, the members of which have systematically different sensations on receipt of the same stimuli, do in some sense live in different worlds. We posit the existence of stimuli to explain our perceptions of the world, and we posit their immutability to avoid both individual and social solipsism."
>
> — *Thomas S. Kuhn*

Transformational Learning

1. Recognize that something is wrong or different. People have experiences that pose a challenge which they convert to a learning opportunity by framing or reframing the problem as they assess what they see, filter it through mental models from past experiences, and use their judgment to make explicit (name) what they see.

2. Explore and search for alternatives. People acknowledge that change is needed and think about what to do about the challenge as they examine and explore the experience. They open themselves to questions and notice feelings, facts, and intuition about the context itself, the people involved, expected ways of acting, anticipated resources, or anticipated impact.

3. Transition. People prepare to adopt new ways and leave the old approaches behind. They mentally test hunches before acting, and investigate many points of view. They decide to accept alternative values, beliefs, assumptions, and norms to those that have been guiding their thinking and actions.

4. Integration, putting the pieces back together, incorporating new views to try out. People experiment in light of new assumptions, learning as they seek reality-based feedback, examine results, and reflect in-and-on the action before, during, and after they experiment.

5. Take definite action. People are no longer tentative about putting new ideas into operation. They assess their actions and draw conclusions and make plans for future learning based on their assessment of both intended and unintended consequences of their actions.

> *"Anomaly appears only against the background provided by the paradigm. The more precise and far-reaching the paradigm is, the more sensitive an indicator it provides of anomaly and hence of an occasion for paradigm change. In the normal mode of discovery, even resistance to change has a use... By ensuring that the paradigm will not be too easily surrendered, resistance guarantees that scientists will not be lightly distracted and the anomalies that lead to paradigm change will penetrate existing knowledge to the core."*
> — *Thomas S. Kuhn*

Group Support and Individual Commitment

1. Deep personal commitment accompanies transformational change. Commitment may be described as "devotion," "dedication," "intensity," or "fanaticism."

2. Reaching and maintaining personal commitment is enhanced by group interaction and support.

3. Studies of social movements describe a "commitment process." Seven steps have been identified (*Luther Gerlach*):

    *   Initial contact with a committed movement participant (usually a pre-existing significant social relationship).

    *   Focus needs of the prospective convert through demonstration by the committed participant of beneficial effects of commitment (redefining the potential convert's needs, desires, or discontents in terms of the new ideology represented by the movement).

    *   Re-education of the prospective convert through group interaction with committed participants, becoming part of a fellowship of learners of the ideology.

    *   A decision to become committed to the ideology (new values, behaviors, self-identity) and to surrender old views.

    *   A commitment event which represents an identity-altering experience and acts as a public bridge-burning act.

    *   Testifying to the conversion experience, telling others and recruiting others to the ideology.

    *   Group support for changed cognitive and behavioral patterns of the converted so they don't revert to old views.

> *"What lies behind us and what lies before us are tiny matters compared to what lies within us."*
> — *Oliver Wendell Holmes*

> *"I know of no more encouraging fact than the unquestionable ability of man to elevate his life by conscious endeavor."*
> — *Henry David Thoreau*

> *"The past, the present, and the future are really one—
> they are today."*
> —*Harriet Beecher Stowe*

> *"Your life is what your thoughts make it."*
> —*Marcus Aurelius*

> *"Let your interests be as wide as possible, and let your
> reactions to the things and persons that interest you be
> as far as possible friendly rather than hostile."*
> —*Bertrand Russell*

> *"A child is like the inexperienced birdwatcher for
> whom every bird is a first. The adult is the experienced
> veteran who approaches each sighting with a highly
> complicated set of expectations and a great deal of
> experience against which to check what he sees; every
> field identification for him is structured by these past
> experiences."*
> —*Harry L. Miller*

5 ADULT EXPERIENCE
interests and values

> "Human beings find less rest in idleness than in a change of occupation. If you scoff at the idea, just try it. Instead of collapsing in an easy chair, try tackling your hobby. Or write that neglected letter, or help Johnny to build that radio receiving set. Activity—especially creative activity—is far better recreation than loafing."
>
> —*Gardner Hunting*

Life Experience and Learning

1. Just by virtue of having lived longer, adults have gathered a greater *volume* of experience than a younger person.

2. Adults have also had a greater *variety* of experience than the youth (few youths have earned their own living, married, had children, taken real community responsibilities, been responsible for the welfare of others, etc.).

3. Because of their life experiences, adults themselves are a rich resource for one another's learning (not as dependent as youth on the vicarious experiences of teachers, experts, textbooks).

4. Adults have a broader foundation of past experience on which to base new learnings.

5. Life experiences form patterns of behavior which require "unlearning" fixed habits of thought. Unconscious dependence on habit can make creative thinking and innovation difficult.

6. Although there are similarities in the experiences of all adults, each adult's particular experiences make that adult unique. No one else has experienced quite the same experiences in quite the same way.

7. Life experience affects readiness to learn. Where adults are in their own "developmental tasks" *(Robert Havighurst)* affects their readiness to learn.

   - Developmental Tasks of Early Adulthood
     1) Selecting a mate.
     2) Getting started in an occupation.
     3) Starting a family.
     4) Rearing children.
     5) Managing a home.
     6) Finding a congenial social group.
     7) Taking a civic responsibility.

---

further study references: 52, 119, 145, 146, 161, 167, 173 **43**

- Developmental Tasks of Middle Age
  1) Relating to one's spouse as a person.
  2) Achieving social and civic responsibility.
  3) Establishing and maintaining an economic standard of living.
  4) Assisting teen-age children to become happy and responsible adults.
  5) Getting to the top of the vocational ladder.
  6) Adjusting to aging parents.
  7) Developing adult leisure-time activities.

- Developmental Tasks of Later Maturity
  1) Adjusting to decreasing physical strength and health.
  2) Adjusting to retirement and reduced income.
  3) Adjusting to death of a spouse.
  4) Establishing satisfactory physical living arrangements.

8. The often conflicting demands of one's life experience in relation to multiple social roles at the same time — child, spouse, parent, worker, homemaker, citizen, friend, organization member, religious affiliate, leisure time user — all impact on one's motivation to learn and change.

9. All adult learning must take into account life experience. Unlike youth for whom learning may be future-oriented and subject-centered, adult learning must be present-oriented and problem-centered. Adults see learning as a process for improving their ability to deal with problems they face now.

10. Another aspect of life experience are the convictions about what one regards as reliable information sources. Information sources may be personal, based on observation and conversation, or impersonal (television, radio, newspapers, and magazines). Generally people come to limit their information sources to those people or media they "trust" and those people or media that confirm already held beliefs.

11. People identify themselves with various groups and govern their behavior to some extent by what they think others will think: members of the family, friends, peers, co-workers, fellow church members, or persons in their racial or ethnic groups.

Adult Interests

1. Interests may be considered the fuel that supplies the energy that gives zest and vitality to life. Kindred interests are the cement with which relationships are built.

2. There is *never nothing* to do. Every person is literally surrounded by more opportunities for involving and satisfying interests than anyone could possibly take advantage of in a hundred lifetimes.

3. Boredom and loneliness are the result of lack of interests, or loss of interests, and result in bad feelings, a sense of powerlessness to help oneself, estrangement from others, and lead to depression and alienation. Bad feelings tend to cause us to think of how bad we feel and in

that way make us feel worse. The painful feelings of loneliness tend to drain the internal strength necessary to handle stress. Talking to a lonely person does not give permanent relief, nor does excessive sleep or endless, mindless TV watching. Loneliness is overcome by action, actively pursuing interests.

4. In general, the things we like most at 25 years of age are liked better and better with increasing age, and the things we liked least at 25 are liked less and less.

5. There is a slight decrease in total volume of interests from the twenties to the fifties, but this decrease is largely in physical activities.

6. Patterns of interests tend to change somewhat with normal shifts in focus of concern that take place during the several phases of the life cycle.

7. Some sort of balance between old interests and new interests is desirable. New interests provide excitement, adventure, discovery, learning. Old interests provide continuity, stability, dependable satisfactions.

8. Perhaps the most pervasive and widely shared interest in our society is watching television (the average viewer watches 28 hours a week; by age 65 the average viewer sees nine full years of TV).

- Television may be viewed for three reasons:

    1) *To learn.* TV, through educational programming, provides opportunities to learn for those seeking new knowledge.

    2) *To be entertained.* Most TV programming is designed to entertain, help the viewer to relax, release tension, divert thought, laugh.

    3) *To escape boredom and loneliness.* This is a mis-use of TV. The "plug-in drug," as it has been called in this context, can never provide an answer to boredom or loneliness. The TV addict for four, five, six or more hours a day slips into a predominantly alpha state — a state that occurs when someone is relaxed, passive, unfocused and not paying attention to anything.

- Why excessive television watching does not enable one to escape boredom and loneliness:

    1) TV is a passive process (requires nothing of the viewer, no thought, no action, though it gives the illusion of involvement).

    2) TV distorts reality (creates an artificial world that to the TV addict *becomes* the real world.

    3) TV immobilizes or physically limits the viewer (one sits and watches).

    4) TV gives the viewer no lasting feeling of value or accomplishment (watching pros perform may make one feel inferior, particularly because the work and hours of practice to succeed are not shown).

5)   TV does not build the strength we need to handle life's stress (life's problems can't be handled with a turn of a switch).

6)   TV *creates* loneliness (by cutting us off from interaction with others).

9.   Interests may be classified as those that give immediate pleasure and those that give long term enjoyment *(Edward E. Ford)*.

Immediate Pleasure Interests	Long Term Enjoyment Interests
Sensuous Do not last Take little or no work Are short and quick	Pleasurable Last for longer periods Take work Lead you to make an effort when you would rather not
Do NOT lead to involvement and self-worth	Lead to love, involvement, worth and positive self-image
Do not build character and strength needed to handle stress later	Build confidence and internal strength to handle stress of life
Do not give lasting good feelings but feel great momentarily Temporary good feelings	Will give us lasting good feelings and more complete sense of self-fulfillment

Adult Values

1.   Values, along with attitudes, interests, beliefs, feelings, are the mix from which adult motivation is derived.

2.   Values in American Society *(Jacob Getzels)*

   • Sacred values (which we pay lip service to):
   1) Democracy
   2) Individualism
   3) Equality
   4) Human Perfectibility

   • Secular Values (day to day operating values)

Traditional Values	Emerging Values
Work-Success Ethic ———————————————→	Sociability
Future-time Orientation ——————→	Present-time Orientation
Independence or Autonomous Self ——→	Group Conformity
Puritan Morality ————————————→	Moral Relativism

3.   Forces Affecting Value Formation

   • Our deepest values are formed in childhood prior to the teens.

   • Forces affecting value formation:
   1) Family
   2) Friends

  3) Church/Religion
  4) Schools
  5) Books (especially textbooks)
  6) Community/Neighborhood
  7) Media (especially television)
  8) Music

4. Impact of Societal Influences on Generation Values *(M. E. Massey)*

Current Age of Adult	Childhood Years of Value Formation	Some Influences on Value Formation
80's	1910's	World War I
70's	1920's	Prohibition Teapot Dome Model T/Airplane Family Closeness
60's	1930's	Depression
50's	1940's	World War II Family Disintegration Mobility
40's	1950's	Prosperity/Affluence Permissive/Indulged childrearing Advent of Television
30's	1960's	Space Program Civil Rights Vietnam Computers
20's	1970's	ERA Drugs Watergate

5. Valuing is *(Raths and Simon)*

 ● Prizing one's beliefs and behaviors
  1) Prizing and cherishing
  2) Publicly affirming, when appropriate

 ● Choosing one's beliefs and behaviors
  3) Choosing from alternatives
  4) Choosing after consideration of consequences
  5) Choosing freely

 ● Acting on one's beliefs
  6) Acting on choice
  7) Acting with a pattern, consistency and repetition

6. Values clarification is a process of identifying and clarifying one's values. A full value must have all seven of the above criteria. If even one of the criteria is missing, it is not a full value but only a partial value or a value that is being formed by the person. Partial values include desires, thoughts not acted on, opinions, interests, aspirations, beliefs, attitudes, etc.

APPLICATION WORKSHEET

Twenty Things I Love To Do

"An Introduction to Helping Adults Learn and Change" by Russell D. Robinson, PhD

1. **List below twenty things you love to do:**

ITEM	RANK	SYMBOL	WHEN
1.			
2.			
3.			
4.			
5.			
6.			
7.			
8.			
9.			
10.			
11.			
12.			
13.			
14.			
15.			
16.			
17.			
18.			
19.			
20.			

2. In the SYMBOL column, after each item place the following symbols as they apply:

   $ If it costs $5.00 or more when you do it.

   A   If you prefer to do it alone.

   P   If you prefer to do it with other people.

   AP   If you do it either alone or with others.

   PL   If it requires planning to do.

   N5   If the item would not have been on your list 5 years ago.

3. Now, in the RANK column, rank (from 1 to 5) what you consider the five most important items.

4. In the WHEN column, indicate next to each activity "when" (day, date) it was last engaged in.

5. Continue marking in the SYMBOL column, after each item, the following symbols as they apply:

   R   If an element of risk (physical, emotional, intellectual) is involved.

   I   If it involves intimacy.

   C   If it is an activity that others might judge conventional.

   CH   If you would like to see this on your children's list.

   PU   If you believe a Puritan would consider this a waste of time.

   B   If you want to become better at doing it.

   L   If you would like this on the list of the person you love most.

   F   If you think the item will NOT appear on your list five years from now.

6. Discuss your responses in a small group.

> "Youth is not entirely a time of life—it is a state of mind. It is not wholly a matter of ripe cheeks, red lips or supple knees. It is a temper of the will, a quality of the imagination, a vigor of the emotions. . .Nobody grows old by merely living a number of years. People grow old only by deserting their ideals. . .You are as young as your faith, as old as your doubt; as young as your self-confidence, as old as your fear; as young as your hope, as old as your despair. In the central place of each heart, there is a recording chamber; so long as it receives messages of beauty, hope, cheer and courage, so long are you young. When the wires are all down and your heart is covered with the snows of pessimism and the ice of cynicism, then, and then only, are you grown old."
>
> —*Douglas MacArthur*

Ethical Development

1. Stages of Intellectual and Ethical Development (*William Perry*)

    *   Dualism (world viewed in polar terms)
        1) Belief in absolute right and wrong
        2) Perceives diversity of opinions and uncertainty which is regarded as unwarranted confusion from poorly qualified sources but certain The Answer can be found
        3) Accepts diversity and uncertainty but considers this temporary ("we/they don't have the answers yet")

    *   Relativism (individual believes that anything can be right or wrong depending on the situation)
        4) Uncertainty and diversity of opinion is seen as legitimate ("anyone has a right to his opinion")
        5) All knowledge and values exist in context ("no right or wrong except in particular situation")
        6) Individual believes in a relativistic world with personal commitment to ideas, rather than the authority giving the ideas

    *   Commitment (finding one's own place through personal choice and commitment)
        7) Individual makes initial commitment to knowledge, ideas, values, beliefs
        8) Individual experiences the implications of commitment and explores the relationships between and among knowledge/ideas; values/beliefs, and responsibility
        9) Individual experiences the affirmation of identity among multiple responsibilities and realizes commitment as an ongoing, unfolding activity in everyday living

> *"Whatever you would make habitual, practice it; and if you would not make a thing habitual, do not practice it, but accustom yourself to something else."*
> —*Epictetus*

Bill of Rights for Adult Learner

1. A democratic nation is possible only with a knowledgeable populace actively committed to the general welfare and alert to opportunities for personal growth and development and continued learning.

2. Adults bring to each learning situation a lifetime of experience. They bring with them their beliefs and values, their hopes and dreams, their fears and concerns. They have the right to learn.

further study references: 52, 125, 158

3. In 1991, the Coalition of Adult Education Organizations which consists of twenty-six national associations and groups sharing a common interest in enhancing the field of adult and continuing education throughout the United States, drafted a bill of rights as follows:

    *   The right to learn regardless of age, gender, color, ethnic or linguistic background, marital status, the presence of dependents, disability, or financial circumstances.

    *   The right to equal opportunity for access to relevant learning opportunities throughout life.

    *   The right to educational leave from employment for general, as well as vocational or professional, education.

    *   The right to financial aid and educational services at levels comparable to those provided for younger or full-time learners.

    *   The right to encouragement and support in learning subject matter that the learner believes will lead to growth and self-actualization.

    *   The right to a learning environment suitable for adults to include appropriate instructional materials, equipment, media, and facilities.

    *   The right to have relevant prior experiential learning evaluated and, where appropriate, recognized for academic credit toward a degree or credential.

    *   The right to participate or be appropriately represented in planning or selecting learning activities in which the learner is to be engaged.

    *   The right to be taught by qualified and competent instructors who possess appropriate subject-matter knowledge, as well as knowledge and skills relating to the instructional needs of adults.

    *   The right to academic support resources, including instructional technology, that can make self-directed or distance learning possible.

    *   The right to dependent care and related structures of social support.

    *   The right to individualized information and guidance leading to further study.

Adult Load, Power and Margin

1.   The key factors of adult life are the *load* the adult carries in living, and the *power* which is available to him to carry the load. *Margin* is the ratio between load and power *(Howard McClusky)*

$$\frac{\text{POWER}}{\text{LOAD}} = \text{MARGIN}$$

This formula clearly suggests that the greater the power in relationship to the load the more margin will be available. A margin of 1.0 is just breaking even, less than 1.0 is a crisis, and more than 1.0 provides a margin to meet the emergencies of life and engage in learning.

(McCluskey has also presented the formula in reverse with the load as the numerator and power as the denominator. In this conception, a ratio of close to 1.00 represents the verge of breakdown, but a ratio of .50 to .80 represents a margin of life space in which to maneuver.)

Definitions of terms:

● Load Factors:

1) *External*—tasks involved in usual requirements of living such as those connected with family, work, civic obligations and the like.

2) *Internal*—expectations set by the individual for himself.

● Power Factors:

1) *Physical*—strength, stamina, energy, health

2) *Social*—ability to relate to others

3) *Mental*—ability to think, reason

4) *Economic*—money, position, influence

5) *Skills*—what the individual knows how to do

● Margin:

1) The load-power ratio changes and adjusts throughout the adult years with changes in any of the power or load factors.

2) That person has the most margin who perceives a power of choice over a range of relevant alternatives.

3) More margin can be gained by decreasing load or by increasing power.

4) Margin is reduced by decreasing power (such as loss of income) or by increasing load (enrolling in an adult education class).

"*We live in deeds, not years, in thoughts, not in figures on the dial; we should not count time by heart-throbs. He most lives who thinks most, feels the noblest, acts the best.*"

—*Philip James Bailey*

further study references: 148, 167, 206

APPLICATION WORKSHEET

My Load, Power and Margin

"An Introduction to Helping Adults Learn and Change" by Russell D. Robinson, PhD

MY LOAD FACTORS:	MY POWER FACTORS:
Obligations and responsibilities:	Physical:
	Social:
	Mental:
Expectations and goals:	
	Economic:
	Skills:

MY MARGIN: Does power exceed load? _____

Are there ways I could increase my power? _____

Are there ways I could decrease my load? _____

"Give instruction to a wise man, and he will be yet wiser: teach a just man, and he will increase in learning."

—Proverbs

"No truth is really taught by words, or interpreted by intellectual and logical method; truth must be lived into meaning, before it can be truly known."

—Horace Bushnell

"Is a musician made by his teacher? He makes himself a musician by practising what he was taught. The conscientious are successful."

— Mary Baker Eddy

"A teacher affects eternity; he can never tell where his influence stops."

—Henry Brooks Adams

6 ADULT TEACHING
helping others learn

> "As we come to understand more about learning and teaching styles and how the mind operates, I believe we will improve mental health and self understanding as well as increase learning. Learning styles and teaching styles have already revealed much to us and continued research will undoubtedly reveal more. This thrust can lead to the revitalization of 'the noblest of the professions.'"
> — Anthony F. Gregorc

The Adult Educator in a Social System

1. An adaptation of the model of *Getzels* and *Guba*:

Social System ⟨

Adult Education Unit ———— Role ———— Role Expectations

Adult Educator ———— Personality ——— Need/Dispositions

⟩ Role Behavior

2. The social system is the cultural or community and organizational context in which the adult education unit or institution and the adult educator functions.

3. Institutional factors affecting role behavior:

    - Institutional Climate:
      Authoritarian ——————————————————— Democratic
      Domination ——————————————— Self-determination
      Regulation ——————————————————— Autonomy
      Distrust ———————————————————————Trust

    - Formal Structure:
      Organization chart and lines of authority and responsibility.

    - Informal Structure:
      Social networks, power centers, friendship groups.

    - Institutional Goals and Program Requirements.

4. Personal factors affecting role behavior:

    ● Education, previous experience, professional identification of adult educator.

    ● Dominance needs, acceptance needs, achievement needs of adult educator.

    ● Other social roles of adult educator, e.g., spouse, parent, citizen, church worker, community leader, etc.

    ● Personal goals.

5. Role behavior depends upon both the person (adult educator) and situation in which he functions (adult education unit or institution).

No One Can Change Another Person

1. You may help another, you may influence another, you may have some impact on another, but the only person who can change a person is the person himself.

2. The "teacher" is not so much a purveyor of knowledge, of the right, the good, that which will "save" another, but, rather, a helper, a facilitator, an encourager of another's finding the knowledge for himself.

3. The first step in helping another is to establish a relationship. In fact, the nature of the relationship between the helper and the learner may have a greater impact on learning than any other single factor.

4. The teacher's expertise in helping lies in the ability to create an environment or situation in which another will be encouraged, or helped to learn. *i.e.,* to discover and try new skills, knowledge and attitudes.

5. The learner is in control of his own learning.

> *"What one knows is, in youth, of little moment; they know enough who know how to learn."*
> —*Henry Brooks Adams*

Creating a Learning Environment

1. Perhaps the most important role of the teacher of adults is to create a learning environment, an "adult atmosphere" for learning, a climate of mutual respect, a friendly, informal, supportive atmosphere.

2. In a non-threatening situation, adults can be helped to diagnose their own needs for learning; they can discover for themselves what they most need to learn, and they can be involved in planning and conducting their own learning.

3. "Adult-like" facilities can be an advantage, but the most important factor is an "adult-like" psychological environment of mutual respect where adults are recognized as responsible and self-directing.

further study references: 28, 156, 168, 190

4.   The learning environment includes:

- The program goals and purposes prescribed by the institution.

- The institutional resources (room, furnishings, equipment, materials)

- The group or class (interactions of group members with each other) and particularly the degree of group cohesion

- The teacher as an individual (perceived credibility, warmth, expertise, etc.)

- The teacher's style of teaching and use of methods and materials

5.   The teacher often has little or no control over program goals and institutional resources, as these are pre-set conditions determined by the employing institution. Although the group or class membership is also pre-determined (teachers rarely get to choose whom they have in their classes), the teacher may cultivate cohesion and interactions among the group. The teacher's personality is somewhat set, but a teacher by his actions can foster warmth and credibility. Teacher style is the variable most in control of the teacher — how the role of teacher is carried out, and the use of methods and materials.

6.   Teaching styles.

Highly content centered style	Content centered style	Mixed style	People centered style	Highly people centered style

- Highly content-centered teaching style:

   1) Teacher conceives self as quite set, demanding, concerned with subject matter and in getting specific tasks done.
   2) Teacher assigned to the group, relationship distant, impersonal, formal.
   3) Materials are major carrier of program, used to present facts and information.
   4) Methods are formal, impersonal, few social activities.

- Highly people-centered teaching style:

   1) Teacher conceives self as flexible, permissive, interested in stimulating discussion and seeing others grow.
   2) Teacher selected by the group, relationships close, personal, informal.
   3) Materials incidental to program, used primarily to present problems.
   4) Methods are flexible, informal, and social activity included.

- Other styles on the continuum suggest modifications in degree.

7. A conceptualization of teaching style — appropriate for particular types of groups and programs *(A. A. Liveright)*

TYPE OF GROUP	TYPE OF PROGRAM		
	Skill Programs	**Understanding Programs**	**Attitudinal Programs**
High Group Cohesion	Content-centered teaching style	Mixed Style	Highly people-centered teaching style
Intermediate Group Cohesion	Content-centered teaching style	Mixed Style	People-centered teaching style
Low Group Cohesion	Highly Content-centered teaching style	Content-centered teaching style	Mixed style

Definitions:

High Group Cohesion—Group has met as a group over period of time, had previous experience as a group in educational programs, has frequent communication, homogeneous membership, and member and leader roles already delegated and set.

Low Group Cohesion—Members have never met as a group before and have had no previous experience as a group in educational programs, have little or no communication outside, not homogeneous, and have no roles set or designated within group.

Skill Programs—Programs with a single and objective concern, of limited scope, answer-giving in nature, with simple and definite goals set by institution.

Attitudinal Programs—Programs with deep and ego-involving concerns and of broad scope, problem-solving in nature, complex and flexible goals set by or amended by the group.

Understanding Programs—Elements fall between skill and attitudinal.

> *"The Tao unifies the parts. . . . The sage rests in the solution of things, and is dissatisfied with what is not a solution."*
> — *Lao-tzu*

> *"The true teacher defends his pupils against his own personal influence. He inspires self-trust. He guides their eyes from himself to the spirit that quickens him. He will have no disciple."*
> —*A. Bronson Alcott*

further study references: 198, 304

8. Creating the Climate for Learning *(Robert Mager)*

- Purpose of all instruction: "the intent to send students away from instruction with at least as favorable an attitude toward the subject taught as they had when they first arrived." *(Mager)*

- People learn to avoid things they are hit with. If conditions for learning are unpleasant, people will avoid the situation, avoid learning, and may learn to hate the subject.

- Need is to accentuate positive conditions and consequences in the learning situation and eliminate the negative, aversive conditions and consequences.

- Aversive conditions to be eliminated:

    1) Conditions which cause students fear and anxiety, distress, tension, foreboding, worry or disquiet, anticipation of the unpleasant.

    2) Conditions which cause frustration, blocking, or interference with student's desire to learn.

    3) Conditions which cause humiliation and embarrassment, causing lowering of a student's self-respect and self-esteem, making him uncomfortable or self-conscious or shaming, debasing or degrading him.

    4) Conditions which cause boredom.

- Positive conditions which create a climate for learning:

    1) Acknowledging students' responses, whether correct or incorrect, as attempts to learn and following them with accepting rather than rejecting comments.

    2) Providing instruction in increments that will allow success most of the time.

    3) Providing enough sign posts so that the student always knows where he is and where he is expected to go.

    4) Giving the student some choice in selecting and sequencing the subject matter.

    5) Relating new information to old, within the experience of the student.

    6) Treating the student as a person.

    7) Providing instructional tasks that are relevant to your objectives and letting your student know what the objectives are.

> *"Every man has the right to feel that 'because of me was the world created.'"*
>
> —*Talmud*

Andragogy vs. Pedagogy

1. "Andragogy" is a word coined by *Malcolm Knowles* from the Greek word *aner* (with the stem *andr-*) meaning "man" and means "the art and science of helping adults learn" as distinguished from "pedagogy" (from the Greek stem *paid-* meaning child) which is the art and science of teaching children.

2. The Andragogical Process *(Malcolm Knowles)*

    • The establishment of a climate conducive to adult learning.

    • The creation of an organizational structure for participative planning.

    • The diagnosis of needs for learning.

    • The formulation of directions of learning (objectives).

    • The development of a design of learning activities (plan).

    • The operation of the learning activities (implementation).

    • The rediagnosis of needs for learning (evaluation).

3. A comparison of andragogy and pedagogy:

ELEMENTS	PADAGOGICAL Teacher-Directed Learning	ANDRAGOGICAL Self-Directed Learning
Climate	Formal authority-oriented, Competitive Judgmental	Informal, mutually respectful Consensual, Collaborative, Supportive
Planning	Primarily by teacher	By participative decision-making
Diagnosis of Needs	Primarily by teacher	By mutual assessment
Setting Goals	Primarily by teacher	By mutual negotiation
Designing a Learning Plan	Content units, Course syllabus, Logical sequence	Learning projects, Learning content sequenced in terms of readiness
Learning Activities	Transmittal techniques, Assigned readings	Inquiry projects, independent study, experimental techniques
Evaluation	Primarily by teacher	By mutual assessment of self-collected evidence

further study references: 166, 167, 168, 169, 326

Communication and Helping

1. Communication may be defined as the mutual exchange of information and understanding. Experts tell us that as much as 70 percent of our communication efforts are likely to be misunderstood, misinterpreted, rejected, disliked, or distorted! We communicate at a 30 percent efficiency rate, yet the average person spends 80 percent of his or her waking hours in some form of communication!

2. A Communication Model

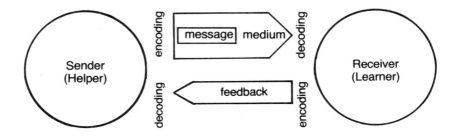

   Communication is a two-way process and occurs only in a relationship. It involves:

   - The sender's perception of the receiver
   - The receiver's perception of the sender
   - Each person's perceptions of the message (words and meaning)
   - The receiver's response to the medium of delivery
   - The sender's response to the feedback

3. Helping is a Communication Process *(Ronald Havelock)*

   - Providing help to others is basically a communication process. As a teacher, or any professional rendering any sort of help for a client, you can analyze your situation in terms of four basic elements:
     1) The helper system (you as sender of message)
     2) The learner system (the person or people you want to help)
     3) The message (the kind of help you want to provide)
     4) The medium (how you want to get the message across; *e.g.*, personal act, group discussion, film, demonstration, etc.)

> *"And these words, which I command thee this day, shall be in thine heart: and thou shalt teach them diligently unto thy children, and shalt talk of them when thou sittest in thine house, and when thou walkest by the way, and when thou liest down, and when thou risest up."*
>
> *—Deuteronomy*

4.   Characteristics of ideal teacher-helpers (*Allen Tough*)

   • They are warm, loving, caring, and accepting of the learners.

   • They have a high regard for the learners' self-planning competencies and do not wish to trespass on these.

   • They view themselves as participating in a dialogue with learners as equals.

   • They are open to change and new experiences and seek to learn from their helping activities.

5.   It is said we learn and remember after a month:

   • 14%   of what we hear
   • 22%   of what we see
   • 30%   of what we watch others do—demonstrations or modeling
   • 42%   of sensory redundancy—rituals that repeat seeing, hearing and doing important skills or concepts
   • 72%   of movies of the mind—learning is linked to remembered or imagined life experiences of the learner
   • 83%   of performance of a life challenge activity—first-time or demanding action that applies the new meaning
   • 92%   of what we teach others

> "When people view themselves as competent and able, their sense of being deserving and their ability to receive what they want expands. A self-fulfilling prophesy works on their behalf. Their anticipation and faith in what's possible accelerates proportionately. It is as if infinitesimal but courageous acts, even just a sliver of a positive thought, become the potent seed they themselves plant. In time this seed bears fruit. With this fruit, their faith in themselves expands. At the end of an intense day's workshop, one woman said, 'I suddenly realize how capable I am. I must have forgotten—or looked the other way. But a moment ago, I experienced my own capabilities <u>as me</u>.'"
> —*Marsha Sinetar*

6.   Listening is as important as effective speaking. Though we spend hundreds of school hours learning to read, write and speak, we spend almost no time learning how to listen.

further study references: 38, 40, 297

7. Effective listeners listen with an understanding attitude. They take into account the problems of listening and realize that, to a large extent, one listens with one's experience. Following are some of the rules for perceptive listening:

- Listen to understand what is meant, not to ready a reply, contradict, or refute.

- Know that what is meant involves more than the dictionary meaning of the words that are used. It involves the tone of voice, the facial expression, the over-all behavior of the speaker.

- Be careful not to interpret too quickly. Look for clues as to what the other person is trying to say, putting yourself in the speaker's shoes, looking at the world as the speaker sees it, accepting the speaker's feelings as facts that have to be taken into account-- whether the listener shares them or not.

- Put aside your own views and opinions for the time being. Realize that you cannot listen to yourself inwardly at the same time you listen outwardly to the speaker.

- Control your impatience because listening and thinking are faster than talking. We speak at 125-175 words a minute but think at 500 to 800 or more words a minute. The effective listener does not jump ahead of the speaker...what is said next may not be what the listener expects. Capitalize on the thought-speech differential by using this time to mentally summarize, organize main points, integrate speaker's information with previously known facts, etc.

- Do not prepare an answer while listening. Get the whole message before deciding what to respond.

- Be interested and alert and show it. This stimulates the speaker and improves one's ability to communicate.

- Do not interrupt. Ask questions to secure more information and find areas of agreement rather than to trap the speaker or force the person into a corner.

- Expect the speaker's language to differ from the way you would say the "same thing." Do not quibble about words or style but try to get at what is meant.

- Provide feedback, summing up what you understand the other to be saying. If your interpretation is not accepted or there is misunderstanding, the matter can be cleared up immediately. "So, what you're saying, Miss Jones, is..."

- Avoid negative feedback (put-downs, solution giving, etc.) that blocks further communication.

Teaching/Learning Styles

1. Carl Jung observed that man normally experiences the world through four modes: Sensing, thinking, feeling and intuition. Sensation is the reality function—it tells us that something is. Thinking is the logical function—it tells us what that something is. Feeling enables us to make a value judgment about the object (whether we like it). Intuition, the method of relating to the world through hunches and guesses, enables us to see the possibilities inherent in the object. Intuition and sensation are conflicting modes of perceiving the world. Thinking and feeling, which are ways one analyzes the world, also conflict. Persons who are strong in one function tend to be weak in its opposite, but everyone has potential for all four functions.

FOUR TYPES OF LEARNING STYLES

Author	FEELER	THINKER	DOER	INTUITOR
Carl Jung	Feeling-directed (Feeling)	Intellect-directed (Thinking)	Body-directed (Sensing)	Intuition-directed (Intuiting)
David Kolb	Divergers Imaginative	Assimilators Theoretical	Convergers Practical	Accommodators Intuitive
Anthony Gregorc	Abstract Random	Abstract Sequential	Concrete Sequential	Concrete Random
Bernice McCarthy	Innovative learners	Analytical learners	Common Sense learners	Dynamic learners
Ned Herrmann	Limbic right brain	Cerebral left brain	Limbic left brain	Cerebral right brain

SOME CHARACTERISTICS OF

FEELERS	THINKERS	DOERS	INTUITORS
Seek meaning	Seek facts	Seek practical	Seek possibilities
Need involvement	Expert knowledge	Learn by doing	Creative
Like sharing ideas	Like ideas, concepts	Like hands-on	Relish change
Like discussion	Theories, paradigms	Concrete things	Self-discovery
Intense feelings	Like lectures	Rely on senses	Trial-and-error
Catch mood, nuance	Logical thinker	Action-oriented	Flexible
Need affiliation	Need achievement	Need power/influence	Risk taking
Past-oriented	Linear time view	Present-oriented	Future-oriented
Spontaneous	Deliberative	Pragmatic	Idealistic
Empathetic	Rational	Directional	Visionary
Introspective	Weighs alternatives	Results-oriented	Original
Loyal	Objective	Seek perfection	Adaptive

CRITICISMS OFTEN HEARD ABOUT

FEELERS	THINKERS	DOERS	INTUITORS
Impulsive	Verbose	Short-sighted	Unrealistic
Manipulative	Indecisive	Status seeking	"Far out"
Over-personalize	Over-cautious	Self-involved	Fantasy-bound
Sentimental	Over-analyze	Act too fast	Scattered
Postponing	Unemotional	Lack trust in others	Out-of-touch
Guilt-ridden	Non-dynamic		Fanatic
Subjective	Too controlled	Expect too much of others	Impractical
Over-emotional	Over-serious		Disorganized
Conforming	Critical	Dominating	Excitable

 further study references: 12, 105, 122, 178, 225, 279, 280

2. Effective helping relates to teaching and learning styles

    *   Teaching style consists of a teacher's personal behaviors and the communication process used to transmit and receive data from the learner.

    *   *Anthony Gregorc, David A. Kolb, Kenneth and Rita Dunn* and others have studied teaching/learning styles.

    *   Learning style consists of distinctive behaviors which serve as indicators of how a person learns from and adapts to his environment. It also gives clues as to how a person's mind operates.

    *   Teachers tend to communicate in styles that match their own preferred ways of learning and their students tend to be most successful when their learning styles match the teacher's. Where styles are mismatched, students "must work hard to learn," or "learn some and miss some material" or "just tune out."

    *   Knowledge of learning styles is the best argument for varying teaching methods in order to meet the range of learner preferences.

    *   Learning style conceptualizations relate to research on right brain/left brain processing. The two halves of the brain are believed to process information differently. Educational practice traditionally has concentrated heavily on the left brain.

        1) The left brain deals with intellectual, analytic, verbal, logical and sequential processing.
        2) The right brain involves intuitive, visuo-spatial, subjective, unstructured and random open-ended processing.

    *   Kolb identifies four learning styles along a continuum of concrete/abstract in perceiving information and a continuum of reflecting/doing in processing information. Juxtaposing the continuums, four learning styles are created:

        1) Thinking Doers. Those who perceive with their intellect and process actively by doing (Convergers).
        2) Reflective Thinkers. Those who perceive with their intellect and process reflectively by observation (Assimilators).
        3) Reflective Sensor-feelers. Those who perceive concretely with their senses and feelings and process reflectively by observation (Divergers).
        4) Doing Sensor-feelers. Those who perceive concretely with their senses and feelings and process actively by doing (Accommodators).

3. Gregorc, like Kolb, uses the concrete and abstract dimension but he crosses it with a different processing dimension which he labels random/sequential. He thus arrives at his four types of learner styles:

Concrete Sequential Learners (CS)

—CS learners are characterized by the tendency to derive information through direct, hands-on experience. They appreciate order and logical sequence. They like touchable, concrete materials. They look for and follow directions and like clearly ordered presentations and a quiet atmosphere.

—CS teachers like to use workbooks, manuals, demonstration teaching, programmed and computer-assisted instruction, hands-on materials, drill, drawings, models, overheads and well-organized field trips. They expect questions to be responded to correctly and step-by-step directions to be followed exactly.

Abstract Random Learners (AR)

—AR learners are attuned to nuances of atmosphere and mood. They associate the medium with the message and tie to the teacher's manner, delivery and personality to the message being conveyed. They evaluate the learning experience as a whole. They prefer to receive information in an unstructured manner and therefore like activities that involve multi-sensory experiences and busy environments. They prefer freedom from rules and guidelines. They seem to gather information and delay reaction and organize material themselves through reflection to get what they want from the learning experience.

—AR teachers use group discussions, short lectures followed by questions/answers and discussion, movies, television, film strips and assignments that permit reflection time. They expect students to learn from, and respond to, fellow students.

Abstract Sequential Learners (AS)

—AS learners have excellent decoding abilities with written, verbal and image symbols. They have a wealth of conceptual pictures in their minds against which they match what they read, hear, or see in graphic and pictorial form. They like to use reading and listening skills. A picture or symbol is worth a thousand words to them. They prefer substantive, rational and sequential presentations from which they can extract the main ideas. They learn well from authorities and like vicarious experiences. They are not deterred by a dull lecturer if the material is well-organized and meaningful.

—AS teachers use extensive reading assignments, substantive lectures, audio tapes and analytical think-sessions. They expect students to conceptualize ideas and convey them either orally or in writing.

Concrete Random Learners (CR)

—CR learners have an experimental attitude. They get the gist of ideas quickly and make intuitive leaps in exploring unstructured problem-solving experiences. They learn by trial-and-error. They work well by themselves and in small groups. They do not follow assignments exactly but add their own twist. They do not respond well to teacher intervention in their independent efforts.

—CR teachers like to use games and simulations, role playing, independent study projects, problem-solving activities, optional reading assignments, and mini-lectures that set the stage for exploration. They expect students to be creative in developing alternate solutions in problem-solving.

Teacher Effectiveness

1. *Thomas Gordon's* T.E.T. (Teacher Effectiveness Training) system for effective teacher behavior begins with the question: Who owns the problem?

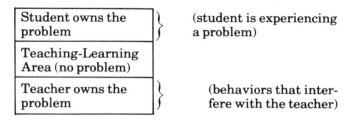

Student owns the problem	(student is experiencing a problem)
Teaching-Learning Area (no problem)	
Teacher owns the problem	(behaviors that interfere with the teacher)

2. Effective teacher behaviors depend on who owns problem.

When the Student Owns the Problem	When the Teacher Owns the Problem
Student initiates the communication	Teacher initiates the communication
Teacher is a listener	Teacher is a sender
Teacher is a counselor	Teacher is an influencer
Teacher wants to help the student	Teacher wants help for himself
Teacher accepts the student's own solution	Teacher has to be satisfied with the solution
Teacher is primarily interested in the student's needs	Teacher is primarily interested in his own needs
Teacher is more passive in the problem solving	Teacher is more active in the problem solving

3. Ways to facilitate communication about *student-owned problems* (Language of Acceptance)

   • Passive Listening (silent listening)

   • Acknowledgment Responses ("Uh-huh," "I see," verbal and non-verbal cues which indicate you are paying attention)

   • Door Openers, Invitations to Talk ("Would you like to talk about it?" "Would you like to say more?")

   • Active Listening (providing feedback)

   Advantages:

   1) Makes students feel their ideas and feelings are respected

   2) Fosters further communication

   3) Defuses feelings and provides cathartic release

   4) Helps students accept their feelings as natural and human

   5) Facilitates identification of the underlying or real problems

6) Starts the problem-solving process going, but leaves the responsibility with students to be their own problem solvers

7) Puts students in the frame of mind of being willing to listen to the teacher by bringing teacher and student into a relationship of greater mutual understanding, mutual respect, mutual caring

8) Carries the risk of being mechanical and sounding phony or manipulative if used as a gimmick without underlying attitudes of worth, empathy, trust and acceptance

● **What is active listening?**

1) Active listening, as opposed to passive listening (silence), involves interaction with the student, and it also provides the student with proof (feedback) of the teacher's understanding.

Example:

Student: "Are we going to have to report to the class?"
(Teacher decodes: He is worried)
Teacher: "You are worried about reporting?"
(If teacher's decoding was incorrect, the student might continue)
Student: "No, it's just that I don't know what kind of report I'm supposed to give and I'm afraid it'll be an individual report."
(Teacher decodes: worried about kind of report)
Teacher: "Oh, you're worried about the kind of report we are going to have."
Student: "Yes, I don't do well on individual reports."
Teacher: "I see, you feel you can do better on group reports?"
Student: "Yes, I'm terrible at speeches."
Teacher: "It'll be a group report."
Student: "What a relief ! I'm not so worried now."

2) The key to active listening is decoding the message and then testing your decoding by providing feedback for the student.

3) The teacher focuses on how the student is feeling about an external situation, not on the external situation itself, keeping the responsibility with the student, not on the outside world. For instance, in the situation where the student says, "My husband never helps me with anything," the teacher focuses on how the sender feels about the situation. She does not place the focus on the husband by saying "He is really a bad guy, huh?"

● **What is required for effective active listening?**

1) The teacher must have a deep sense of trust in students' ability ultimately to solve their own problems.

2) The teacher must be able to genuinely accept the feelings expressed by students, however different from how the student "should" feel.

3) Feelings exist only as of the moment and are often quite transitory. Active listening helps students move from momentary feeling to momentary feeling.

4) Teacher must want to help students with their problems and make time for it.

5) Teachers must be "with" each student who is experiencing troubles, yet maintain a separate identity, that is, teachers must experience the feelings *as if* they were their own, but not let them *become* their own.

6) Teachers need to understand that students are seldom able to start out by sharing the real problem.

7) Teachers must respect the privacy and confidential nature of whatever the student reveals about himself or his life.

4. Twelve roadblocks to communication on student-owned problems (Language of Unacceptance)

- Giving solutions
    1) Ordering, commanding, directing
    2) Warning, threatening
    3) Moralizing, preaching, giving "shoulds" and "oughts"
    4) Advising, offering solutions or suggestions
    5) Teaching, lecturing, giving logical arguments

- Putting-down
    6) Judging, criticizing, disagreeing, blaming
    7) Name-calling, stereotyping, labeling
    8) Interpreting, analyzing, diagnosing

- Soothing
    9) Praising, agreeing, giving positive evaluations
    10) Reassuring, sympathizing, consoling, supporting

- Probing
    11) Questioning, probing, interrogating, cross-examining

- Indirect
    12) Withdrawing, distracting, being sarcastic, humoring.

5. When *the teacher owns the problem,* the teacher tries to modify unacceptable behavior. There are three choices:

- Attempt to modify the learning environment
    (Modifying the learning environment may be all that will be required)

- Attempt to modify the student's behavior
    (By using "I-messages" instead of "You-messages")

- Attempt to modify self
    (By changing the way conflict is handled)

6. Modifying the student's behavior requires a confrontation with "I-messages" not "You-messages."

- "You-messages" throw up the roadblocks to communication.

  1) Solution messages: "You must, and you should, you had better, you do it now. . .!"

  2) Put-down messages: "You always, you never, you're acting like. . ., you dumb. . .!"

  3) Indirect messages: Sarcasm, teasing, "How would you like to take over the class?"

- "I-messages" state how the teacher feels about the behavior and how it affects him.

  Examples:
    "I'm frustrated by this noise."
    "I'm really annoyed when people interrupt me"

  An "I-message" must have three components:

    1) What behavior is creating a problem for the teacher?

    2) What is the tangible or concrete effect on the teacher of this behavior?

    3) What feelings are generated within the teacher because he is tangibly affected?

  Example:
    "When you smoke in class *(description of behavior)*, I'm bothered by the smoke *(tangible effect)* and I'm afraid *(feeling)* I'll start coughing."

- After giving an "I-message" the teacher needs to watch for clues for appropriate follow-up. The student has been told that his behavior is unacceptable, troublesome, or hurtful to his teacher. *If cues indicate student accepts the problem, then the student owns the problem and the teacher can shift to active listening.*

- Why teachers may find "I-messages" difficult

  1) Risk of self-disclosure

  2) Risk of possibility of self-modification

  3) Risk of taking responsibility for your own behavior

7. When "I-messages" don't work, confrontation becomes conflict, and in conflict *both* own the problem, because the needs of both parties are at stake. The teacher must modify his behavior and initiate action to resolve the problem. He has three approaches open to him:

- **Method I. Teacher Wins—Student Loses** *(Authoritarian approach)*

  Results:

—Produces resentment and often strong hostility in the student toward the teacher.

—Produces little motivation in the student to carry out the solution.

—Often requires heavy enforcement on the part of the teacher.

—Inhibits growth of self-responsibility and self-direction and fosters dependence

—Fosters compliance and submission, mainly out of fear, and inhibits cooperation.

—Inhibits creativity, exploration and motivation.

—Fosters low productivity, low morale, low job satisfaction, and a high rate of turn-over (drop-outs).

- **Method II. Teacher Gives In—Student Wins** *(Permissive approach)*

  Results:

  —Can be quick—just ignore the behavior, get rid of conflict by giving in.

  —Produces resentment and hostility in the loser, toward the winner (teachers end up hating students).

  —Fosters in the winners (students) selfishness, lack of cooperation, lack of consideration of others.

  —Makes students lose respect for the teacher, who is seen as weak, incompetent.

- **Method III. No Lose Method. Both Win** *(Problem-solving approach)*

  The six-step process:

  —Defining the Problem (focus of conflict)

  —Generating Possible Solutions (without evaluation)

  —Evaluating the Solutions

  —Making the Decision (by consensus)

  —Determining How to Implement the Decision

  —Assessing the Success of the Solution

  Results:

  —No resentment.

  —Motivation increases to implement the solution.

  —Encourages creative thinking.

  —No need to "sell" the solution.

  —No power or authority is required.

  —Students like teachers, teachers like students.

  —Students become more responsible, more mature.

Ten Commandments for Adult Educators

1. Based on the work of *J. Roby Kidd* as modified by Roger Hiemstra and Burton Sisco.

    ● Thou shalt never try to make another human being exactly like thyself; one is enough.

    ● Thou shalt never judge a person's need, or refuse your consideration, solely because of the trouble caused by the individual.

    ● Thou shalt not blame heredity nor the environment in general; people can surmount their environments.

    ● Thou shalt never give a person up as hopeless or cast the individual out.

    ● Thou shalt try to help everyone become, on the one hand, sensitive and compassionate, and also tough-minded.

    ● Thou shalt not steal from any the rightful responsibilities for determining their own conduct and the consequences thereof.

    ● Thou shalt honor anyone engaged in the pursuit of learning and serve well and extend the discipline of knowledge and skill about learning that is our common heritage.

    ● Thou shalt have no universal remedies or expect miracles.

    ● Thou shalt cherish a sense of humor, which may save you from becoming shocked, depressed, or complacent.

    ● Thou shalt remember the sacredness and dignity of thy calling and, at the same time, thou shalt not take thyself too seriously.

> *"If one thinks back to his own school days, one will probably remember that the good teachers one has had in one's lifetime did not all behave alike or even with great similarity. Rather, each stands out as a person, an individual, some for one reason, some for another. Each had his own peculiar methods, values, and techniques. Good teaching is like that, an intensely personal thing."*
> —*Arthur W. Combs*

Facilitating Adult Learning

1. Principles of Facilitation (*Stephen Brookfield*)

   - Voluntary Participation. Because adults have chosen to engage in the learning activity, they bring their own initial motivation. Effective facilitation must meet those expectations or learners will withdraw.

   - Mutual Respect. Effective facilitation is characterized by a respect for each participant's uniqueness, self-worth, and separateness.

   - Collaborative Spirit. Effective facilitation requires some kind of participatory and collaborative element.

   - Action and Reflection (Praxis). Effective facilitation centers on a continuous and alternating process of investigation and exploration, followed by action grounded on this exploration.

   - Critical Reflection. Effective facilitation aims to foster an attitude of skepticism and examination of assumptions.

   - Self-direction. Effective facilitation aims to assist adults to become self-directed learners.

2. Overcoming student resistance to learning (*Stephen Brookfield*)

   - Ask yourself whether the resistance is justified. Try to sort out the causes of the resistance. Research your students' backgrounds and cultures.

   - Involve students in educational planning. Conduct regular formative evaluation sessions.

   - Explain your intentions clearly. Justify why you think learning is important.

   - Involve former resisters in working with new resisters.

   - Create situations in which students succeed. Accentuate the positive.

   - Encourage peer learning and peer teaching.

   - Don't push too fast. Attend to the need to build trust.

   - Admit that student resistance is normal. Strike a bargain with resisters. Acknowledge students' right to resist.

3. William Glasser describes two approaches to teaching/managing. One he calls boss-management teaching; the other lead-management teaching. The question is, in the learning environment, does the teacher function as a "boss" or as a "leader."

BOSS-Management Teaching	LEAD-Management Teaching
Boss sets task and standards for students; does not compromise; student must adjust	Leader engages students in discussion of quality of work; seeks input; fits job to skill and needs of students
Boss tells rather than shows; rarely asks for input as to how it could be done better	Leader shows or models for the student; seeks student input for a better way
Boss inspects the work; students tend to settle for just enough quality to get by	Leader asks student to inspect and evaluate own work for quality and set criteria
When students resist, boss uses coercion (punishment); students become adversaries	Leader facilitates a fair, friendly, noncoercive, and nonadversarial atmosphere

The Teaching/Learning Transaction

1. Teaching is provided in a "learning environment" but learning is done by the learner.

2. Elements in the "learning environment" with which the teacher is concerned include:

   • Institutional program goals

   • Institutional resources

   • Degree of group cohesion and interaction in class

   • The teacher as an individual

   • The teacher's style of teaching and use of methods and materials (the teaching plan)

3. Into this learning environment each individual learner brings his own unique and individual motivations: needs, perceptions and assumptions, self-concept, feelings, adult life stage, interests, values, life experience and pattern of response to change. And he brings with him some problem about which he believes or hopes that he can receive help in the learning environment.

4.   The transaction may be pictured as follows:

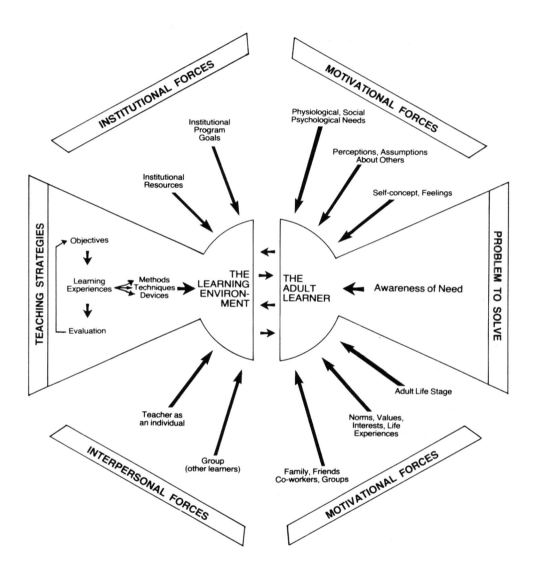

INSTITUTIONAL FORCES

MOTIVATIONAL FORCES

Institutional
Program
Goals

Physiological, Social
Psychological Needs

Institutional
Resources

Perceptions, Assumptions
About Others

Self-concept, Feelings

TEACHING STRATEGIES

Objectives

Learning
Experiences

Methods
Techniques
Devices

THE
LEARNING
ENVIRON-
MENT

THE
ADULT
LEARNER

Awareness of Need

PROBLEM TO SOLVE

Evaluation

Adult Life Stage

Teacher as
an individual

Norms, Values,
Interests, Life
Experiences

Group
(other learners)

Family, Friends
Co-workers, Groups

INTERPERSONAL FORCES

MOTIVATIONAL FORCES

> "There is no happiness in having, or in getting, but
> only in giving."
>
> —Henry Drummond

5.   The "success" of the transaction depends on all of these factors plus the appropriateness of the teacher's help for the learner at whatever point the learner is in the learning process.

THE PROCESS OF LEARNING	HOW THE TEACHER MAY HELP
Awareness of a need or a problem and a desire (want) to do something about it.	• Provide relevant spoken and written information and audio-visual materials. • Provide opportunity to talk about problems with each other.
Active interest, information-gathering, self-inquiry, to find out what might be done.	• Provide classes, instruction, information. • Provide opportunity for learners to seek out information, clarify, digest, discuss. • Provide opportunity to analyze, diagnose and define problem and search for alternate solutions.
Mental trial, developing intellectual insight and a "mental map" of how a solution might work in his situation.	• Provide learners opportunity to think and discuss and explore solutions with others they trust and respect. • Provide safe atmosphere for thinking and talking and making a decision. • Help learners reduce resisting forces of fear and doubt.
Trial practice of new behavior to see if a particular solution really would work in his situation and staying with trial through cognitive dissonance (*know* it's right but it *feels* wrong) until emotional insight is gained (now it *feels* right).	• Provide opportunities to actually try out the new behavior in a safe environment • Provide support and direct help as needed. • Provide encouragement and psychological support. • Provide opportunities for learners to share and support each other.
New behavior has become the way of thinking, feeling, acting.	• Help no longer needed.

> *"Education does not mean teaching people to know what they do not know; it means teaching them to behave as they do not behave."*
>
> —*John Ruskin*

APPLICATION WORKSHEET

Myself as a Teacher

"An Introduction to Helping Adults Learn and Change" by Russell D. Robinson, PhD

I am MOST effective as a teacher of adults when I ---

I am LESS effective as a teacher of adults when I ---

> "*And seeing the multitudes, he went up into a mountain: and when he was set, his disciples came unto him: And he opened his mouth, and taught them. . . and it came to pass, when Jesus had ended these sayings, the people were astonished at his doctrine: For he taught them as one having authority, and not as the scribes.*"
>
> —*Gospel of Matthew*

> "*Education is not a matter of packing articles in a trunk.*"
>
> —*Alfred North Whitehead*

> "*What is it that keeps alive in some people the natural spark of curiosity, eagerness, hunger for life and experience and how may we rekindle that spark when it flickers out? If we ever solve that problem, we will be at the threshold of a new era, not only in education but in human experience.*"
>
> —*John W. Gardner*

7 ASSESSING ADULT NEEDS
starting where the learner is

The Three R's of Adult Learning

1. Relevancy — must make sense to the adult learner.

2. Relationship — must be related to adult learner's needs.

3. Responsibility — adults must assume responsibility for their own learning.

The Felt Need—Key to Learning

1. Learners put themselves in learning situations and learn in order to satisfy felt needs.

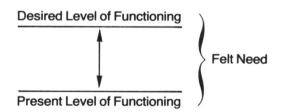

2. These needs may be job-related needs or personal needs or, very likely some combination of both. Job needs are ordinarily tangible and specific in nature, usually recognized, and can be discussed more easily. Personal needs are often less clearly identified and more likely talked about in terms of "people in general."

3. The first step in identifying job-related needs is to be able to describe what one is doing when performing his job. The second step is to describe job performance in detail, listing each of the tasks of which the job is composed and describing the steps in each of these tasks *(task analysis)* and to compare this information with what the learner already knows and is able to do.

Cost-Benefit Considerations

1. When making a decision about whether to participate in a learning experience, a person is primarily interested in two things:
   - What will I get out of it? (benefits)
   - What will I have to put into it? (costs)

2. If a person feels that the benefits are greater than the costs, he will probably become involved. If the costs are greater than the benefits, a person is likely not to get involved.

3. Cost-Benefit questions revolve around such issues as:
   - Time required
   - Nature of learning experience
   - Perceived threat to self-esteem
   - Money required
   - Energy demands
   - Physical comfort

Incentives for Adult Learning

1. People want to gain
   - Health
   - Time
   - Money
   - Popularity
   - Improved appearance
   - Security in old age
   - Praise from others
   - Comfort
   - Leisure
   - Pride of Accomplishment
   - Advancement; business, social
   - Increased enjoyment
   - Self-confidence
   - Personal prestige

2. They want to be:
   - Good parents
   - Social, hospitable
   - Up to date
   - Creative
   - Proud of their possessions
   - Influential over others
   - Gregarious
   - Efficient
   - "First" in things
   - Recognized as authorities

3. They want to do:
   - Express their personalities
   - Resist domination by others
   - Satisfy their curiosity
   - Emulate the admirable
   - Appreciate beauty
   - Acquire or collect things
   - Win others' affection
   - Improve themselves generally

4. They want to save:
   - Time
   - Money
   - Work
   - Discomfort
   - Worry
   - Doubts
   - Risks
   - Personal embarrassment

(Irving Lorge)

Need Assessment Methods

1. Individual assessment

   - Though adults in learning settings are accustomed to having their learning needs decided for them, once they experience the process of assessing their own needs, they prefer this to having someone else decide.

   - The process involves learners in building their own competency models for self-development and then comparing their present situations against the models.

2. Group (Assessment) Discussion

   - Assessing learning needs in small groups in which members help each other to clarify their individual needs enables them to become resources for each other's learning.

   - The process may involve collecting group discussion data on news-print and hanging up the list for all to see so they can "keep track" of their discussion.

3. Questionnaires and Surveys

   - Data gathering devices such as check lists, sentence completion, questionnaires, or organizational or community surveys, may be relatively simple or quite sophisticated.

   - In any case, such devices should be pre-tested, revised to avoid bias, and administered to preserve anonymity.

   - It is important that findings be reported to the population surveyed and that the needs generated be responded to.

4. Systems Analysis

   - Methods of systems analysis, or input/output analysis, may be used to analyze organizations as functioning social systems according to systems criteria such as feedback flow, input/output relationship, and the relationship of systems and subsystems.

5. Organizational or Community Records and Reports

   - Operating records can often indicate trends or give clues to the existence of potential learning needs.

   - Needs are often made apparent as a result of formal studies or research activities conducted by organizations.

6. Professional Literature

   - Often professional journals or articles raise questions or produce new insights that lead directly to an increased awareness of learning needs. A review of professional literature can help identify needs in special fields or activities.

7. Resource Persons

   - Talking to experts in various activities can help gather additional information or gain a different perspective about learning needs.

8. Tests

    - Diagnostic tools may be used to identify specific areas of deficiencies.

    - Tests may be threatening to adults. A climate needs to be established for the test.

    - Tests, obviously, must be appropriate. Some tests may not measure what they are supposed to measure and results would have little value.

9. Analysis and Performance Review

    - A job analysis provides specific and precise information about jobs and performance.

    - It is time-consuming and difficult to do by people not specifically trained in job analysis techniques.

    - Analysis, obviously, must be of current job and current performance.

Involving the Learner in Planning

1. It is the *learner* who learns. It is the learner's needs that are being met (or not met). The learners are in control of their own learning.

2. The effectiveness of a learning program is in direct relationship to the involvement of the learner in its determination, implementation and evaluation *(Malcolm Knowles):*

    - Adults can be helped to *diagnose* their own needs for learning. In non-threatening situations individuals can discover for themselves what they need most to learn.
      —Needs derived from teachers' experience, needs of the agency, or needs of the subject-matter can be negotiated with the learners.

    - Adults can be involved in *planning and conducting* their own learning, translating diagnosed needs into specific educational objectives and designing learning experiences to meet these objectives.
      —Substantive planning (goals, objectives) is primarily the function of the learner.
      —Procedural planning (how to achieve their goals and objectives) may require the help of a resource (expert, teacher) in mutual planning.

    - Adult learners can *evaluate* their own progress toward their learning goals.
      —The student, not the teacher, is the judge of how well the student is doing, whether or not the student's objectives are being met.

3. Adults are often so accustomed to "playing school," having someone tell them what they need to know and whether or not they know it, it may take some practice in self-diagnosis, self-planning, and self-evaluation before learners are confident of their own judgments.

further study references: 38, 94, 168

APPLICATION WORKSHEET

Needs Assessment

"An Introduction to Helping Adults Learn and Change" by Russell D. Robinson, PhD

What method/methods will you use in determining the students' learning needs?

_____

_____

_____

What have you found to be the learners' needs?

SKILL Needs	KNOWLEDGE Needs	ATTITUDE Needs

What are the benefits of learning for the learner? _____

_____

_____

_____

What are the costs of learning for the learner? _____

_____

_____

_____

83

> *"The ideal condition*
> *Would be, I admit, that men should be right by instinct;*
> *But since we are all likely to go astray,*
> *The reasonable thing is to learn from those who can teach."*
>
> —*Sophocles*

> *"What a piece of work is a man! how noble in reason! how infinite in faculty! in form and moving how express and admirable! in action how like an angel! in apprehension how like a god! the beauty of the world! the paragon of animals!"*
>
> —*William Shakespeare*

> *"If you plan for a year, sow a seed.*
> *If you plan for a decade, plant a tree.*
> *If you plan for a century, educate the people."*
>
> —*Kuan-tzu*

8 DESIGN FOR LEARNING
choosing the method

> "A bee puts to shame many an architect in the construction of her cells. But what distinguishes the worst architect from the best of bees is this, that the architect raises his structure in imagination before he erects it in reality. At the end of every labor process we get a result that already existed in the imagination of the laborer at its beginning."
>
> —Karl Marx

Basic Questions in Designing a Learning Experience

1. What is the primary focus of the program?
    - to solve individual needs or problems?
    - to solve group needs or problems?
    - to solve community needs or problems?

2. What is the setting (format) in which the learning will take place?
    - an individual setting?
    - a group setting?
    - a community setting?

3. What will be the primary instructional goals?
    - to inform, disseminate knowledge, develop understanding?
    - to teach skills, new behaviors?
    - to change attitudes, values, opinions, feelings?
    - to encourage creativity?

4. What instructional resources will be available?
    - access to instructors, speakers, panel members, discussion leaders?
    - access to instructional materials and devices?
    - place and facilities?
    - how much time?

5. How many learners will be involved?

A Model of Designs in Adult Education Practice

1. There are nine different designs in the practice of adult education, depending on the transactional mode utilized in learning (the format) and the client focus (primary goals of the learner). *(Robert Boyd and Jerold Apps)*

<table>
<tr><td rowspan="2"></td><td rowspan="2"></td><td colspan="3">CLIENT FOCUS</td></tr>
<tr><td>Individual Change Goals</td><td>Group Change Goals</td><td>Community Change Goals</td></tr>
<tr><td rowspan="3">TRANSACTIONAL MODE</td><td>Individual Learning Format</td><td>A learner utilizing individual resources to improve his knowledge, skills and attitudes.</td><td>A learner utilizing individual resources to improve his ability to help solve group problems.</td><td>A learner utilizing individual help to improve his ability to help solve community problems.</td></tr>
<tr><td>Group Learning Format</td><td>A learner utilizing a group setting to improve his knowledge, skills and attitudes.</td><td>A group concerned with solving group problems and functioning more effectively.</td><td>A group concerned with working to solve community problems.</td></tr>
<tr><td>Community Learning Format</td><td>A learner utilizing a community to improve his knowledge, skills and attitudes.</td><td>A community group working together to solve a group problem.</td><td>A community group or several groups working together to solve community problems.</td></tr>
</table>

Methods

1. Within each general format (individual, group, or community) there are a variety of methods or approaches that may be utilized.

FORMAT	METHODS	DESCRIPTION
Individual	Apprenticeship	under guidance of experienced worker
	Computer-based instruction	interaction with programmed computer
	Correspondence Study	course by mail with correspondence with instructor
	Coaching/Counseling	help as needed
	Directed Individual Study	help from instructor from time to time
	Field Experience	supervised field work
	Independent Reading/Study	learner-initiated systematic reading and study

further study references: 7, 31, 168, 169, 170, 259

FORMAT	METHODS	DESCRIPTION
	Individual Learning Project	learner-initiated use of several resources to accomplish specific learning.
	Observation/Imitation	observing and imitating another's performance
	Programmed Instruction	course outlined step by step, with immediate feedback on learning
	Supervision	help from supervisor
	Tutorial	one-on-one with instructor
Small Group (up to 30)	Class/Course/Training	series over a period of time
	Clinic	diagnosis, analysis and solving of problems
	Clubs/Organized Groups	in almost every club one purpose is education of its members
	Colloquium	an advanced group where research projects are planned and evaluated as they progress
	Committee/Task Force	3 to 7 members with specific task
	Discussion Group	8 to 15 discussing mutual concerns and issues, usually with assistance of discussion leader
	Executive Committee/Boards	5 to 9 members with general overseeing responsibilities
	Laboratory Group	8 to 15 studying their own group processes, usually with trainer or facilitator
	Residential Learning	live-in experience of several days
	Round Table	intensive analysis of a specific problem common to all present
	Seminar	advanced students in specialized study, learning from discussing their projects and experience with each other
	Sensitivity Group	8 to 15 helping each other through self-disclosure and feedback, usually with trainer
	Short Course	abbreviated versions of longer courses, tailored for clientele
	Team	5-7 working and learning together
	Trip/Tour	on site observation and learning
	Workshop	emphasis on work sessions, problem-solving, output

FORMAT	METHODS	DESCRIPTION
Large Group (more than 30)	Assembly	usually for purpose of agreement on some action
	Conference	one or more days to consider topics using a variety of techniques
	Convention	usually several days with total group and smaller group sessions bringing together local members in a district, state or national meeting
	Forum	usually presentation of information followed by audience questions and participation
	Institute	concentrated sessions, usually over several days, for development of knowledge or skill in a specialized area
	Lecture Series	a lecture course with same or different speakers over period of time
	Meeting	one- to three-hour sessions
	Orientation Sessions	to provide information to a new group
	Telecommunications	video or voice-only teleconferencing to several sites
Community	Community Action Groups	for purpose of taking action in the community
	Community Development	a process involving the community in its own development and improvement
	Community Problem-solving Groups	for purpose of solving problem
	Community Projects	for purpose of accomplishing a project
	Exhibits, Fairs	for purpose of displaying wares, accomplishments
	Result Demonstration	for purpose of displaying results

> *"By his ability to reason, his power of memory, and his gift of imagination, man transcends time and space. As marvelous as are the stars is the mind of man that studies them."*
>
> —*Martin Luther King, Jr.*

further study references: 22, 31, 113, 305, 306

Learner Goals

1. The primary focus of the learner (to solve individual, group, or community problems) can be further delineated in terms of particular goals: skills, knowledge or attitudes to be learned.

CLIENT FOCUS	TYPE OF LEARNING (CHANGE) DESIRED			
	Knowledge (Cognitive)	Skill (Psychomotor)	Attitude (Affective)	Creativity
Individual Change Goals	to develop individual knowledge	to develop individual skill	to develop individual attitudes	to develop individual creativity
Group Change Goals	to develop group knowledge	to develop group skills	to develop group attitudes	to develop group creativity
Community Change Goals	to develop community knowledge	to develop community skills	to develop community attitudes	to develop community creativity

Design Considerations

CHANGE DESIRED	SOME BASIC DESIGN CONSIDERATIONS
Knowledge	1. Specify key information. 2. Associate new information with learner's previous knowledge. 3. Help learners review and put information in own words.
Skills	1. Specify clearly skill goals (what, how, when, where, to what degree). 2. Help learners develop, practice ability levels. 3. Provide examples, models.
Attitudes	1. Help learners clarify values, discuss points of view. 2. Emphasize advantages, positives. 3. Help learners empathize with views discrepant to their own. 4. Provide channels for continuing support over long-term.
Creativity	1. Help learner develop a creative mental set. 2. List and record creative ideas. 3. Reward creativity.

> "All education should contribute to moral and physical strength and freedom."
> — *Mary Baker Eddy*

Timetable for Planning

1. **Several months ahead**
   - Determine audience, needs, focus, goals, methods
   - List subjects; develop theme/title
   - Determine price; estimate budget
   - Select coordinator
   - Determine location, dates

2. **A few months ahead**
   - Prepare subjects and resource person lists
   - Invite resource persons
   - Determine and order mailing lists
   - Draft publicity plans; prepare first press release
   - Design brochure; prepare copy

3. **Several weeks ahead**
   - Mail brochures
   - Send out more press releases
   - Order or prepare workbooks, other materials
   - Determine time schedules of resource persons
   - Make A/V requests
   - Contact on-site personnel
   - Establish registration procedures

4. **A couple of weeks ahead**
   - Follow up on publicity
   - Check on all on-site arrangements
   - Send welcome letters to participants
   - Reconfirm resource persons and time schedules

5. **After the event**
   - Prepare final participant list
   - Correspond with resource persons
   - Review evaluation critiques

further study references: 15, 60, 72, 140, 168, 209, 251, 291, 295, 296, 30

What is the primary focus of the program?

_____ to solve individual needs or problems

_____ to solve group needs or problems

_____ to solve community needs or problems

How many learners will be involved? _____

What is the setting or format in which the learning will take place?

_____ individual setting

_____ group setting

_____ community setting

What resources will be available?

Time: _____

Place and facilities: _____

_____

Leadership and resource people: _____

_____

Materials and devices: _____

_____

_____

What will be the primary instructional goals?

_____ to inform, disseminate knowledge, develop understanding

Example(s): _____

_____ to teach skills, new behaviors

Example(s): _____

_____ to change attitudes, values, opinions, feelings

Example(s): _____

_____ to encourage creativity

Example(s): _____

"My eyes already touch the sunny hill, going far ahead of the road I have begun. So we are grasped by what we cannot grasp; it has its inner light, even from a distance—and changes us, even if we do not reach it, into something else, which, hardly sensing it, we already are; a gesture waves us on, answering our own wave."

— *Rainer Maria Rilke*

"If a man doesn't know what port he is heading for, no wind is favorable to him."

—*Seneca*

"The aim of education should be to convert the mind into a living fountain, and not a reservoir."

—*John M. Mason*

"One may walk over the highest mountain one step at a time."

—*John Wanamaker*

9 DEVELOPING OBJECTIVES
choosing the targets

> "Educational objectives become the criteria by which materials are selected, content is outlined, instructional procedures are developed, and tests and examinations are prepared."
>
> —Ralph W. Tyler

A Model for Program Development

Assessment of Learner Needs
What does the learner need?

Evaluation
Did the learner learn?

Overall Learning Goals and Design
What and how will I attempt to teach?

Criteria-Evidence
How will I know I have taught it?

Teaching Plan
What learning experiences need to be provided to accomplish this?

Assess Resources
What resources do I have available for teaching?

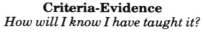

Instructional Objectives
What does the learner need to be able to do?

Preliminaries to Developing Instructional Objectives

1. Some systematic needs assessment is the first step in program planning.

2. On the basis of the needs identified, the teacher can decide on over-all design and goals for the educational program—the general format and the topics, components, that should be included.

3. The teacher needs to identify the criteria or evidence that will show that the learner has learned. The more specific this identification, the greater likelihood that a program will be designed to produce the evidence.

4. The teacher needs to assess resources available: how much time? what kinds of materials? what facilities? what instructional competencies?

Instructional Objectives Must Be Specific

1. Objectives should be brief enough to be remembered.

2. Objectives should be clear enough to be written down.

3. Objectives should be specific enough to be attainable.

Ingredients of an Instructional Objective

1. An objective says something about the *learner*.

   - It does not describe the textbook, the instructor or the kind of learning experience.

2. An objective identifies an *observable behavioral act* or performance of learners. It describes what the learner will be able to do.

   - It does not describe the performance of the instructor.

3. An objective is about *ends* rather than means.

   - It describes how the learner will demonstrate his achievement at the end of the instruction rather than the means to be used to get there.

4. An objective describes the *conditions* (givens, restrictions, limitations) under which the learner will be performing the behavior.

   - It describes what the learner will be able to utilize when performing a behavior (for example, with or without a pocket calculator or open book).

5. An instructional objective includes information about the *level of performance* that will be considered acceptable.

   - Criterion of acceptable performance might include: How many errors will be permitted? How much time will be allowed? What quality will be acceptable?

(Robert Mager)

Attitudinal Objectives

1. Objectives relating to attitudes should be explicitly stated and the design of the learning experiences take into account such objectives.

    Examples:

    *   Student to complete the instruction more interested in the subject than when he began (learner will continue to like the subject).

    *   Student to follow failure with another immediate attempt to succeed (persistence).

2. Unless attitudinal objectives are made explicit, provisions for their attainment are not likely to be included in the learning experiences planned.

> "A great many people think they are thinking when they are really rearranging their prejudices."
> —*Edward R. Murrow*

Types of Performance Objectives

1. Discrimination

    *   Knowing when to do it, knowing when it is done.

    *   Discrimination means being able to tell the difference between two or more things.

2. Problem-Solving

    *   How to decide what to do.

    *   Problem-solving is the process of finding the trouble and deciding what needs to be done next.

3. Recall

    *   Knowing what to do, knowing why to do it.

    *   Recall or remembering is the ability to recall to thought information when it is needed.

4. Manipulation

    *   How to do it.

    *   Manipulation refers to ability to do a skill. Learned by practice.

5. Speech

    *   How to say it.

    *   Speech skills are required in the performance of many tasks.

> "For the things we have to learn before we can do them, we learn by doing them."
> —*Aristotle*

Language of Instructional Objectives

1. *Use* words open to fewer interpretations

   - to write
   - to recite
   - to identify
   - to differentiate
   - to solve
   - to construct
   - to compare

   Avoid words open to many interpretations

   - to know
   - to understand
   - to really understand
   - to appreciate
   - to fully appreciate
   - to grasp the significance of
   - to believe

2. Examples of action verbs for various objectives:

Knowledge Objectives	Skill Objectives	Attitude Objectives
to analyze	to adjust	to accept
to categorize	to arrange	to adopt
to classify	to assemble	to advocate
to compare	to build	to bargain
to contrast	to calculate	to challenge
to describe	to conduct	to cooperate
to differentiate	to construct	to defend
to distinguish	to demonstrate	to dispute
to evaluate	to detect	to endorse
to explain	to execute	to examine
to formulate	to fix	to justify
to identify	to install	to persuade
to investigate	to isolate	to question
to list	to lay out	to resolve
to modify	to operate	to select
to outline	to perform	
to prepare	to produce	
to rank	to solve	
to recall	to sort	
to report		
to state		

3. Sometimes a teacher may find it virtually impossible to state an important objective in behavioral terms. In that event, the teacher should state the objective, even if not in measurable terms. Such an objective, though inexactly stated, may still serve as a "direction for learning" for the learner and a help in planning for the teacher.

APPLICATION WORKSHEET

Constructing Instructional Objectives

"An Introduction to Helping Adults Learn and Change" by Russell D. Robinson, PhD

	DESCRIPTION Learner will be able to- (describe action or performance)	CONDITIONS Conditions under which performance will take place	CRITERION Level of Performance (speed, accuracy, quality)
SKILLS			

KNOWLEDGE			

ATTITUDES			

97

"I find the great thing in this world is not so much where we stand, as in what direction we are moving: To reach the port of heaven, we must sail sometimes with the wind and sometimes against it—but we must sail, and not drift, nor lie at anchor."

— *Oliver Wendell Holmes*

"In every department, one must, in the first place, begin again as a child; through patient interest in the subject, take pleasure in the shell until one has the happiness to arrive at the kernel."

—*Johann W. von Goethe*

"The teacher is one who makes two ideas grow where only one grew before."

—*Elbert Hubbard*

DEVELOPING TEACHING PLANS
sequencing and selecting

Course Development

1. There are three phases in course development *(Robert Mager)*

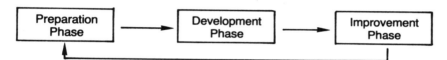

Preparation Phase → Development Phase → Improvement Phase

2. The preparation phase (needs, goals, objectives) has been considered in the earlier chapters.

    *   Assessing Adult Needs
    *   Designing the Adult Learning Experience
    *   Developing Instructional Objectives

3. The development phase (developing the teaching plan) includes the following components:

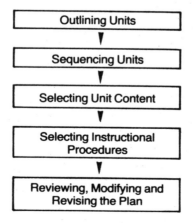

Outlining Units
↓
Sequencing Units
↓
Selecting Unit Content
↓
Selecting Instructional Procedures
↓
Reviewing, Modifying and Revising the Plan

4. The improvement phase (evaluation) is the third stage in course development and will be considered in a subsequent chapter. It involves a specific plan to see how well the course meets the objectives and a willingness to make modifications before the course is offered again.

Outlining Units

1. Course development begins with outlining instructional units in terms of the instructional objectives (what will the student be able to do to demonstrate new skills, knowledge or attitudes at the completion of each unit).

2. A unit may take several sessions to complete, or more than one unit may be completed in a single session. The important thing is that units directly relate to the instructional objectives.

Sequencing Units

1. After the units have been identified, preliminary sequencing of the units is carried out.

2. There are six guidelines for sequencing instructional material:

   • Sequence from the general to the specific. Do the "big picture" first, and then move from the big picture to the details or elements.

   • Sequence in terms of learner interest. Start with those aspects where student interest already exists.

   • Sequence in a logical way, especially in a way that will seem logical *to the learner.*

   • Sequence skills so some useable skills are learned even if student leaves the course before completing it.

   • Sequence skills used frequently first, so those skills that will be used most often are taught sooner, and less-used skills later.

   • Sequence to allow practice of the entire task. By the end of the program, have an opportunity to put the bits and pieces together.

Selecting Unit Content

1. Content is determined by the question: What does the student need to know in order to perform this task (achieve the instructional objective)?

2. Rarely does a teacher feel that there is enough time available to teach all that he would like to teach. There are always time constraints for every course, workshop, institute, conference—a limited number of hours of instructional time available.

3. To avoid expending time on less important or less vital elements and not having sufficient time for the most crucial elements, the instructor must early separate what he would like to teach (if time were unlimited) into what the learner "must know" and what would be "nice to know."

further study references: 45, 168, 215, 2?

4. All "must know" (and "must be able to do" and "must attitudes" as well) should be included *as content* for the learning experience. Some "nice to knows" can be added to the extent that time is available. Remember, the learner has a lifetime ahead of him to learn more.

Selecting Instructional Procedures

1. There are many terms used in the literature to describe instructional procedures. One typology uses the terms "methods," "techniques," and "devices." *(Coolie Verner)*

    - Methods (also called formats, modes, approaches)

       Methods identifies "the ways in which people are organized in order to conduct an educational activity." Methods may be grouped as individual methods, group methods, and community methods.

    - Techniques (also called methods, procedures, strategies)

       Techniques are "the ways in which the instructional agent establishes relationship between the learner and the learning task." Techniques may be designed to help the learner acquire information, acquire a skill, apply knowledge, develop creativity, change an attitude.

    - Devices (also called instructional materials, teaching aids)

       Devices are "instructional aids that extend or increase the effectiveness of methods and techniques, but which cannot themselves instruct." They may range from books to simulators, from film to working models, from chalkboards to video tapes.

2. The following chapter provides information on a variety of techniques and devices and suggests purposes for which they may be utilized.

3. Selecting the appropriate instructional procedures involves:

    - Choosing the techniques and devices most appropriate to the instructional objectives.

    - Choosing those techniques and devices which are most practical from among those that are appropriate.

Reviewing, Modifying and Revising the Overall Plan

1. After outlining and sequencing the instructional units and selecting content and procedures, the plan can be reviewed as a whole, using criteria such as:

    - Is there continuity from one lesson to the next?

    - Will the student spend most time engaged in activities directly relevant to objectives?

    - Can the procedures selected actually be implemented with the time and facilities available?

    - Is there a logic to the whole course, from lesson to lesson?

- Is the amount of learning attempted appropriate for the amount of time available (not too much or too little)?

- Will the learner always be informed of where he is and how far he has come?

2. Modified and revised, the plan is ready for try-out.

3. The lesson plan is a guide to the way students and teacher will spend the time in a session, rather than a document that precisely dictates what must happen during each instructional minute. There must be room for flexibility.

4. Planning is a highly ordered, rational, step-by-step, logical activity, carried on by the teacher *before* the session, but *teaching* is an art requiring quite different qualities, a high degree of flexibility, spontaneity, sensitivity and inspiration in working with learners.

Detailing the Instructional Unit

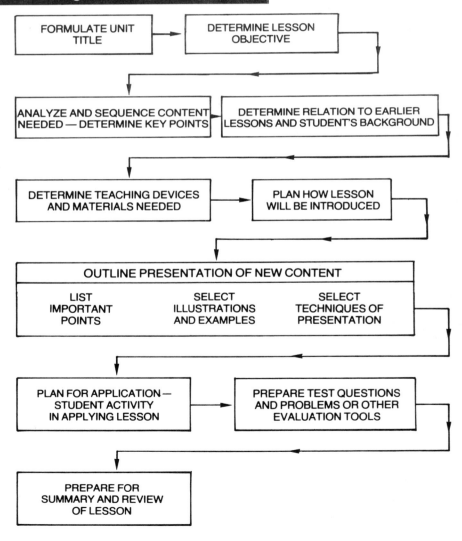

APPLICATION WORKSHEET

Outline for an Instructional Unit

"An Introduction to Helping Adults Learn and Change" by Russell D. Robinson, PhD

Title of Unit: _____

OBJECTIVE Learner will be able to---	CONTENT Key Points to emphasize	TECHNIQUES AND DEVICES Learning Experiences to be provided	ESTIMATED TIME

103

"*Treat people as if they were what they ought to be and you help them become what they are capable of being.*"
—*Johann W. von Goethe*

"*And it came to pass, that after three days they found him (Jesus) in the temple, sitting in the midst of the doctors, both hearing them, and asking them questions.*"
—*Gospel of Luke*

"*All men by nature desire knowledge.*"
—*Aristotle*

"*My thoughts are my company; I can bring them together, select them, detain them, dismiss them.*"
—*Walter Savage Landor*

1 TECHNIQUES AND DEVICES
variety and appropriateness

> "The teacher is not the giver of knowledge. He is not the full reservoir from which the pupils are to draw supplies of fact and theory at will. He is the awakener and quickener of the knowledge-getting faculties in his pupils. He is the artesian-well driver, connecting the power of the pupil with the resources of the world beneath and above."
>
> —John H. Vincent

A Wise Selection

1. With so many techniques and devices to choose from, the instructor can be like a gourmet cook, carefully choosing just the right combination to achieve the results desired.

2. There is no excuse for the habitual overuse of lecture as the primary and often only technique.

3. What is the *best* teaching technique? There is no answer to this question. It depends on your *purpose*.

4. Techniques may be classified by purpose, although a particular technique may have usefulness for other purposes as well.

   - Techniques to impart knowledge
   - Techniques to teach a skill
   - Techniques to change attitudes
   - Techniques to encourage creativity

5. Most techniques are best used in combination with other techniques.

6. Many techniques require other particular techniques as follow-ups.

7. What is the worst teaching technique? The one that is used all the time, whatever it is! Variety is the spice of the learning situation.

8. This chapter suggests more than 40 techniques and as many devices for the convenience of the program planner and presents 10 different general meeting room arrangements.

Instructional Techniques to Impart Knowledge

1. Techniques appropriate for ONE RESOURCE PERSON PRESENTATIONS to inform, give information, disseminate knowledge, develop understanding:

TECHNIQUE	DESCRIPTION	ROOM ARRANGEMENT
Committee Hearing	Questioning of a resource person by a panel of interviewers for extemporaneous responses.	
Film	One-way organized presentation	
Interview	Questioning of a resource person by an individual on behalf of audience.	
Lecture, Speech	One-way organized formal presentation of information or point of view by resource person	
Lecture with Group Response Team (Audience Reaction Team)	Several group representatives interrupt resource person at appropriate times for immediate clarification of issues	
Screened Speech	Sub-groups develop questions they wish resource person to address extemporaneously	

> *"No one can make you feel inferior without your consent."*
>
> —*Eleanor Roosevelt*

> *"And Jesus went about all the cities and villages, teaching in their synagogues, and preaching the gospel of the kingdom. . ."*
>
> —*Gospel of Matthew*

further study references: 13, 20, 65, 168, 194,

2. Techniques appropriate for SEVERAL RESOURCE PERSON PRE-SENTATIONS to inform, give information, disseminate knowledge, develop understanding:

TECHNIQUE	DESCRIPTION	ROOM ARRANGEMENT
Colloquy	Panels of 3 or 4 resource persons and 3 or 4 representatives of the audience discussing issue.	
Debate	Conflicting views stated by each resource person and clarified further by argument between them.	
Dialogue	Informal, conversational discourse between 2 resource persons.	
Dramatic Presentation	Prepared play or skit to inform.	
Interrogator Panel	2 to 4 resource persons questioned by 2 to 4 interrogators.	
Panel Discussion	Panel of 4 to 7 resource persons carry on a discussion of an issue before an audience (informal discussion "overheard" by audience).	
Symposium	3 to 6 speeches or lectures presented in turn by resource persons on various phases of a single subject or problem.	

> "Man has come to control all other forms of life because he has taken more time in which to grow up; when he takes still more time, and spends this time more wisely, he may learn to control and remake himself."
>
> — *Will Durant*

3. Techniques appropriate as FOLLOW-UPS to presentations of one or more resource persons to involve the audience:

TECHNIQUE	DESCRIPTION	ROOM ARRANGEMENT
Buzz Groups	Sub-groups of 4 to 6, with 4 to 6 minutes to discuss particular issue or question raised by resource person.	
Chain Reaction Forum	Sub-groups discuss presentation and formulate questions to be asked resource person.	
Forum	Free and open question/discussion period immediately following a lecture.	
Group Discussion	Sub-groups of 10—20 discuss problems or issues raised, for 15—30 minutes.	
Huddle Groups	Pairs or triads (2-3 persons/groups) discuss specific issue for 2 to 3 minutes.	
Listening Team	3—4 members in audience are designated to listen and raise questions after presentation.	
Question Period	Opportunity for any in audience to directly question speaker.	
Reaction Panel	Panel of 3 or 4 react to presentation by panel discussion.	
Reaction Symposium	3 or 4 persons in turn give their reaction to presentation.	
Screening Panel	3 or 4 persons screen questions raised by audience (on cards) before presenting questions to resource person.	

further study references: 13, 20, 65, 168, 194, 230, 245, 28

Instructional Techniques to Teach a Skill

1. Techniques appropriate to teach a skill or change a behavior:

TECHNIQUE	DESCRIPTION
Action Maze	Programmed case study involving a series of decision points with options at each point.
Behavior Modeling	A model or ideal enactment of desired behavior by instructor or video.
Case Study	Presentation of a problem or case for a small group to analyze and solve.
Demonstration	Instructor verbally explains and performs an act, procedure or process.
Games, Structured Experiences	Under leadership of instructor, learners participate in a "game" requiring particular skills.
Simulation	Learners learn skills in a setting that simulates the real setting where skills are required.
Teaching/Learning Team	Working cooperatively, small groups of 3—6 persons each teach and help each other develop skills.

2. Techniques appropriate for FOLLOW-UP and practice of skills:

TECHNIQUE	DESCRIPTION
Application Projects	Performance contracts, check lists, specific exercises to apply learnings "back home."
Drill	Practice beyond the point needed for recall to produce automatic response.
Practice	Repeated performance of a skill under supervision of instructor, and then without supervision.

Instructional Techniques to Change Attitudes

1. Attitudes are most likely to be changed in a context of free and open discussion, in a climate of trust. In such a climate assumptions and attitudes can be examined with less threat and defensive behavior.

2. Techniques appropriate to change attitudes, values, opinions, feelings:

TECHNIQUE	DESCRIPTION
Circle Response	Question posed to members of a group seated in a circle, each person in turn expressing a response.
Exercises, Structured Experiences	Planned activities in which learners participate, after which they discuss feelings and reactions.
Field Trips, Tours	Experiencing or viewing actual situations for first hand observation and study.
Games	Experiencing a game and discussing its application to real life.
Group Discussion	Circle face to face mutual exchange of ideas and opinions by members of small groups (8—20) on problem or issue of mutual concern for 10—40 minutes, depending on size of group.
Process Group (T-Groups, Laboratory Groups)	Circle of 8—12 people studying themselves in process of becoming and being a group.
Role Playing	Impromptu dramatization of a problem or situation, followed by discussion.
Sensitivity Group	Circle of 8—12 people helping each other through self-disclosure and feedback.
Simulation	Experience in a situation as near real as possible, followed by discussion.
Skit	Short rehearsed dramatic presentation, followed by discussion.
Values Clarification	Structured experiences designed to help learner examine values held

further study references: 13, 20, 123, 168, 194, 230, 287, 290, 3

3. Virtually every technique listed above requires PROCESS TIME, opportunity for learners to evaluate, discuss, and process the experience.

Instructional Techniques to Encourage Creativity

1. Techniques appropriate to encourage creativity, new ideas, thinking in new paths:

TECHNIQUE	DESCRIPTION
Brainstorming (ideation: idea inventory)	Free flowing and uninhibited sharing and listing of ideas by a group without evaluation or consideration of practicality; object is to generate as many creative ideas as possible.
Affinity Diagram	Generate major themes from a large number of ideas, opinions, and issues: 1. Individuals write ideas on cards (or Post-it notes) 2. Place all cards on table (or Post-its on newsprint wall) 3. In silence, move cards into related groups; don't discuss 4. Creat "header cards" for groupings 5. Draw lines connecting headers, sub-headers, with cards beneath them
Nominal Group Process (Delbecq Technique)	A specific procedure for a group of 5 — 8 people for maximum idea generation and narrowing the range of ideas: 1. Each person makes his own list of ideas (5 — 10 minutes) 2. Master list is made on newsprint in round robin fashion as each contributes one idea to list until **all** ideas are on master list (10 — 15 minutes) 3. Clarification (but not discussion) of items on master list (15 minutes) 4. Each person chooses 5 items from the master list without discussion (5 minutes) 5. Each person ranks 5 items and accords value points (5 for first, 4 for second, 3 for third, 2 for fourth, 1 for fifth) 6. "Votes" (value points) are recorded for each item on master list. 7. Ideas receiving the most points are discussed.
Quiet Meeting (Quaker Meeting)	15 — 60 minute period of reflection and limited verbal expression by group members; periods of silence and spontaneous verbal contributions.
Self-analysis and Reflection	Time allocated for personal reflection and opportunity to relax and examine learning alone.

> *"Well done is better than well said."*
> —*Benjamin Franklin*

Instructional Devices

1. There are many instructional devices (also called instructional aids or instructional materials) available today.

2. Below are grouped such devices from the most concrete and experiential, in directly involving the learner, to the more abstract, relying on verbal symbols (words) alone.

3. Note that audio-visual aids are *not* more effective than experiential devices.

INSTRUCTIONAL DEVICES

CONCRETE

- Worksheets, observation guides, manuals, workbooks
- Models, mock-ups, objects, specimens
- In-basket exercises, structured experiences, games, critical incidents, case studies
- Stem sentences, discussion starters, discussion guides

Experiential

- Skits, plays, puppetry, simulations
- Video-tapes, television
- Films, slide films with sound

Audio-visual

- Audio-tapes, records, radio, recording and playback devices
- Slides, film strips, projected still pictures
- Overhead projection, opaque projection of charts, diagrams, graphs, photographs, etc.
- Photographs, maps, posters, drawings, charts, etc.
- Chalkboards, cork boards, flipcharts, flannel boards, hook and loopboards

Visual or audio

- Information briefs, summaries, handouts, study guides, programmed texts
- Publications, books, pamphlets, newspapers, magazines, articles, anotated reading lists

Written

ABSTRACT

further study references: 168.

Room Arrangements

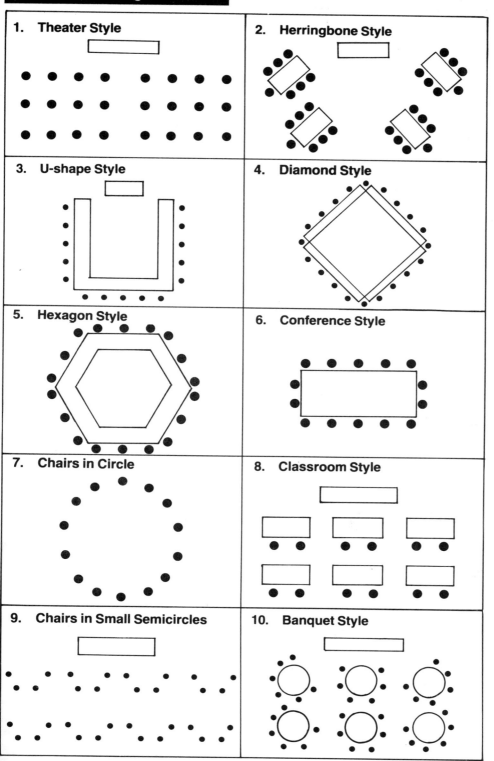

1. **Theater Style**

2. **Herringbone Style**

3. **U-shape Style**

4. **Diamond Style**

5. **Hexagon Style**

6. **Conference Style**

7. **Chairs in Circle**

8. **Classroom Style**

9. **Chairs in Small Semicircles**

10. **Banquet Style**

On the Use of Questions

There are three types of questions that may be asked in a classroom or discussion group context.

1. Questions of *Fact*

   - A question of fact requires a factual answer; there is one "right" answer to such a question.

   - Such questions are used to check knowledge of the facts.

2. Questions of *Interpretation*

   - A question of interpretation asks for *meaning*. What does this statement *mean?* It may seek
     —the meaning of a phrase
     —the meaning of a sentence
     —the meaning of some action or event
     —the meaning of a writer

   - These are "why" questions, about which there may be several opinions. There is no one correct answer. These are questions that can be *discussed*.

   - Such questions are used to understand meaning.

3. Questions of *Evaluation*.

   - A question of evaluation asks the student to what extent the ideas under discussion have application to his own life, his own personal experience, and his standard of values.

   - Questions of evaluation differ from interpretive questions in that they ask the student for his own viewpoint rather than to interpret what an author means.

   - These are "what would you do?" or "what would you have done?" questions.

   - Such questions are used to encourage application.

On Group Discussions

1. Three uses of discussion

   - Gathering information

   - Exchanging ideas and viewpoints

   - Solving problems

2. Suggestions for group discussion leaders:

   - Arrange group in circle, so each person can see every other person.

   - Let all stay seated during discussion, including leader. Keep i informal.

   - See that everybody knows everybody else. At first gathering, g around the circle, each introducing himself, or have members pai off and introduce each other. As a newcomer joins group late introduce yourself to him and him to the group.

- Have chalkboard, chalk and eraser or flip chart ready for use in case of need. Appoint a "chalk secretary" if the subject-matter and occasion make it desirable.

- In opening, emphasize: *Everyone* is to take part. If one single member's view fails to get out in the open, to that extent the discussion falls short.

- Emphasize: *No speeches,* by leader or group member. No monopoly. After opening statement, limit individual contributions to a minute or so.

- Make your own preparation for the discussion. Think the issues through in advance. Aim to establish connections between ideas of background materials, and experience and ideas of group members.

- At outset get a sharply defined question before the group. Have three or four alternatives put on board if you think this will help. "Which do you want to start with?" "Is this question clear?"

- In general, don't put questions to particular group members, unless you see that an idea is trying to find words there anyway: "Mrs. Brown, you were about to say something." Otherwise: "Let's have some discussion of this question. . ." "What do some of the rest of you think about this?" 'We've been hearing from the men. Now how do you women feel about this?" "What's been the experience of you folks in your community in this connection?" Etc.

- Interrupt the "speech maker" as tactfully as possible: "While we're on this point, let's hear from some of the others. Can we save your other point 'til later?"

- Keep discussion on the track; keep it always directed, but let the group lay its own track to a large extent. Don't groove it narrowly yourself.

- Remember: the leader's opinion doesn't count in a discussion. Keep your own view out of it. Your job is to get the ideas of others out for an airing.

- If you see that some important angle is being neglected, point it out: "Bill Jones was telling me last week that he thinks... What do you think of that?"

- Keep the spirits high. Encourage ease, informality, good humor. Let everybody have a good time. Foster *friendly* disagreement. Listen with respect and appreciation to all ideas, but stress what is important, and turn discussion away from what is not.

- Take time every ten minutes or so to draw the loose ends together: "Let's see where we've been going." Be as fair and accurate in summary as possible.

- Close discussion with summary—your own or the secretary's. Call attention to unanswered questions for future study or for reference back to speakers. Nourish a desire in group members for continuing study and discussion.

On Cooperative Learning

1. Cooperative learning, developed by *David W. and Roger T. Johnson*, is a way of learning cooperatively by working together in contrast to traditional methodolologies of individual learning or competitive learning.

2. Basic elements of cooperative learning

    - Structures for positive interdependence and a sense of mutuality

    - Requires face-to-face interaction (talking, discussion, problem solving)

    - Establishes personal commitment and responsibility (individual accountability)

    - Utilizes interpersonal and small group skills (cooperative group and communication skills)

    - Includes structured reflection and feedback (group processing)

3. Organizing a cooperative learning group

    - Clear and specific objectives (for both content and collaborative tasks)

    - Small groups (2, 3 or 4 persons)

    - Heterogeneous groups

    - Seating "knee to knee and eye to eye"

    - Materials to be shared

    - Assigned roles (reader, recorder, checker, praiser, encourager of participation, etc.)

    - Provide task assistance to clarify, elaborate

    - Intervene to teach collaborative skills

    - Provide time for processing and closure

> *"Do not worry about holding high position; worry rather about playing your proper role."*
> — *Confucius*

4. Examples of cooperative learning methodologies

- Jigsaw: each student (with a partner) reads and studies part of a selection, then practices teaching the section with a new partner (student who studied the same section from another group), then teaches what has been learned to the other members of the group. Each then quizzes group members until satisfied that everyone knows all parts thoroughly.

- Learning Partners: student turns to a neighbor to ask something about the lesson, explain a concept just taught, how to do something just taught, or summarize three most important points, etc.

- Drill Partners: students drill each other on the facts they need to know until both partners know and can remember them all.

- Problem Solvers: groups work on problem, each student contributing part of solution.

- Report Groups: students research a topic together, each checking at least one different source and writing at least three notecards of information, then write report together.

- Summary Pairs: students alternately read and orally summarize paragraphs.

- Elaborating and Relating Pairs: students elaborate on what they are learning and relating it to what they already know about the subject.

> "The best thing to do behind a person's back is to pat it."
> —*Franklin P. Jones*

> "There are no problems we cannot solve together, and very few that we can solve ourselves."
> — *Lyndon Baines Johnson*

> "Love not what you are but only what you may become."
> — Cervantes

> "The man who knows what he is, whence he is, whither he is going, how he is related to the world and his fellows, is the cultured man."
> —Thomas Davidson

> "First, be sure that your means for doing good are equal to your motives; then, judge them by their fruits."
> — Mary Baker Eddy

> "Most of the shadows in this life are caused by standing in one's own sunshine."
> —Anonymous

2 CONDUCTING EVALUATION
instructional improvement

> "The basic purpose of evaluation is to stimulate growth and improvement. Whatever other worthy purposes exist are only facets of the all-inclusive effort to assess present conditions as a basis for achieving better ones. Evaluation that does not lead to improved practice is sterile."
>
> —Homer Kempfer

Why Evaluate?

1. For determining effectiveness of program.
2. For purposes of instructional improvement.
3. For purposes of program justification/accountability.

Elements to be Evaluated

1. The program design: was it appropriate?
2. The teaching and instructional resources: were they adequate?
3. The students: what knowledge, skills and attitudes were learned?
4. On-the-job results: did the instruction result in changed behavior back on-the-job or at home?

Two Types of Evaluation

1. Formative Evaluation

   - Evaluation conducted *during* an educational program so that immediate feedback may be provided and appropriate changes made.
   - Especially important during developmental phases of a program.

2. Summative Evaluation

   - Evaluation conducted *after* an educational process has been completed so that judgments and comparisons might be made of its effectiveness.
   - Basis of changes next time program is offered.

---

study references: 60, 64, 65, 111, 168, 245, 330

119

Levels of Evaluation

1. **Reaction** (How did the learners like the program?)

   • Frequently used anonymous reactions; sometimes called "happiness scales" because they measure feelings of learners, not specific learning.

   • Learners mark "checksheets" responding to questions or items on a rating scale (often 1-5) representing degrees of "like" (excellent, very good, good, fair, poor) by each participant. Might ask such general questions for rating as, How do you rate the content? How do you rate the instructor? How were the meeting facilities, luncheon, etc.? Or more specific items. In developing checksheets, determine what it is you want to find out and phrase statement to be rated. Design the form so it can easily be tabulated and quantified.

   • Sheets usually also provide for "open-ended" comments as well (What did you like? How would you suggest the program be improved? Other comments.)

2. **Learning** (What concepts, facts, and skills were learned?)

   • Learning involves skills (how to do), knowledge (facts, concepts, understanding), and attitudes (valuing of the learning).

   • Observe and rate performance of skills. Check knowledge with paper and pencil posttests, or better, with pretests of knowledge followed by posttests at conclusion of sessions.

3. **Behavior** (What changes in behavior on the job or elsewhere resulted from the learning experience?)

   • Requires systematic appraisal of on-the-job performance both before and after the learning program. Appraisal may be made by the person receiving the instruction, the person's supervisor, person's subordinates or peers. Appraisal is conducted some time after completion of the learning program (3-6 months).

4. **Results** (What were the tangible results of the program in terms of improved quality, greater efficiency, improved customer service, etc.?)

   • Learning programs are sponsored for employees in order to obtain particular results such as improved morale, increase in production, reduced turnover or whatever. Result measurement requires prior data collection (benchmarking) and data collection some time later (3-6-9 months) following the learning activity.

5. **Experimental Research Design** (Comparisons with control groups)

   • A more formalized design for evaluation of learning, behavior or results (levels 2, 3, and 4 above) embodying pre- and post-testing of matched control groups and comparisons between those who participated in the learning experience and a matched group of those who did not.

Requirements for an Evaluation Plan

1. **Statement of objectives**

   - Evaluation is possible only if there has been a clear statement of the objectives of the educational activity in terms of behavior changes in the people who are doing the learning.

   - What criteria or evidence will indicate the achievement of the results sought?

2. **Source of evidence**

   - Only those people whom you try to reach can provide proof of success or failure.

   - What will you need from them to provide the evidence?

3. **Representative sample**

   - Those people who actually provide the evidence of success must be representative of all whom you tried to reach.

   - A carefully drawn but representative sample (where each has equal chance of being drawn—such as "every tenth name") can provide essentially the same evidence as the total group.

4. **Data Collection**

   - The methods of obtaining evidence must be appropriate to the kinds of information being collected.

   - Questions must be worded carefully to obtain reliable unbiased data. A pre-test of questionnaire is most desirable.

   - Basic methods of data collection
     1) Questionnaires
     2) Interviews
     3) Tests
     4) Observation

5. **Data Analysis and Use**

   - Decide how you will analyze and use evaluation results before evaluation is done.

   - Collect, arrange and analyze the data

   - Interpret and draw conclusions from the data

   - Compare the conclusions to the stated objectives

   - Record recommendations for changes in the next program

Evaluation Techniques

1. Some evaluation techniques used depending on primary instructional goal.

Knowledge	Skill	Attitude

Written Tests:
    multiple choice
    true-false
    matching
    sentence completion
	Performance Tests:
	    perform skill
	    practical application
	    use equipment
	    use simulators
		Instruments:
		    attitude scales
		    "feel statements"
		    journals
		    diaries

Written Essays:
    analyze, evaluate
    compare, discuss
	On-the-job Observations:
	    performance behaviors
	    standards of performance
		Role Playing:
		    expression of attitudes

Oral Presentations:
    present to group
    oral tests
	Product Reviews:
	    evaluate product
		Exercises:
		    evaluate actions

Two Evaluation Models

1. The CSE (Center for the Study of Evaluation at UCLA) Model:

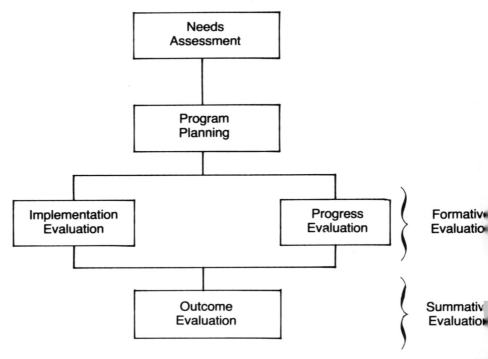

further study references: 45

- Needs Assessment

  1) *Determine Unmet Needs*—gathering data to show what needs are not being adequately met by existing programs.

  2) *Select Objectives*—determining objectives which a program is intended to meet.

  3) *Rate Objectives*—determining how to combine and weight ratings of objectives by constituent groups.

- Program Planning

  4) *Explore Alternative Resources*—determining which resources will be most effectively and most feasibly utilized in meeting the program objectives.

  5) *Prepare Evaluation Design*—deciding how to ascertain whether or not program objectives are met.

  6) *Develop Data Collection Instruments*—designing the instruments that will be used to collect evaluation data.

- Implementation Evaluation

  7) *Check Administrative Functions*—devising and utilizing an instrument to record when administrative tasks, such as promotion, registration, scheduling, are performed.

  8) *Classroom Observation*—observing a class in session to determine whether or not the instructor is dealing with the subject matter in the course outline.

  9) *Review Program*—reviewing a program proposal to determine whether or not the program is being implemented as it was designed.

- Progress Evaluation

  10) *Report Student Achievement*—reporting the average scores achieved by students after one month into a new program.

  11) *Establish Feedback Procedures*—implementing methods for making data which measures student progress available to teachers so they can see how well students are doing.

  12) *Prepare Interim Report*—reviewing data and writing a report indicating the extent to which the program is meeting objectives.

- Outcome Evaluation

  13) *Reassess Needs*—reviewing a summary report to determine what needs are now being adequately met and which are still unmet.

  14) *Evaluate Achievement of Participants' Goals*—review the results of the program to decide whether or not the program should be continued.

2. The Stake Model

- Developed by *Robert E. Stake* of University of Illinois at the Center for Instructional Research and Curriculum Evaluation.

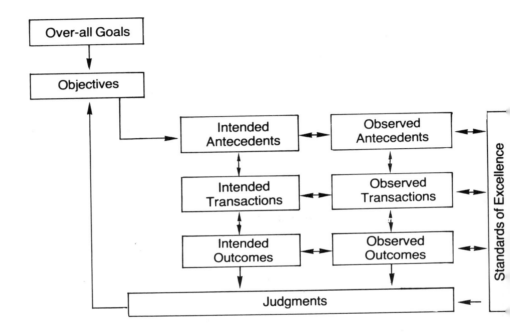

- An antecedent is any condition existing prior to teaching and learning that may relate to outcomes.

- Transactions are the countless encounters of students with teacher, student with student, author with reader, the succession of engagements which comprise the process of education

- Outcomes are the impacts of instruction, such as the abilities achievements, attitudes, and aspirations of students resulting from an educational experience, as well as its impact on teachers and administrators, wear and tear on equipment and costs.

- This model suggests there are two principal ways of processing descriptive valuation data:

    1) Finding contingencies (relationships) among Antecedents Transactions and Outcomes

    2) Finding congruence between Intents and Observations. To be fully congruent the intended antecedents, transactions, and outcomes would have to come to pass.

- Data collected are compared to accepted standards of excellence and evaluative judgments are made.

APPLICATION WORKSHEET

A Plan for Evaluation

An Introduction to Helping Adults Learn and Change" by Russell D. Robinson, PhD

Program to be evaluated: _____

From whom will evidence (data) be collected: _____

_____

_____

OBJECTIVE (Learner to be able to---)	DATA NEEDED (Evidence)	METHOD (How collect)

How will I analyze the data? _____

_____

How will I use the data? _____

_____

_____

"The conception of individual fulfillment and lifelong learning finds no adequate reflection in our social institutions. For too long we have paid pious lip service to the idea and trifled with it in practice. If we believe what we profess concerning the worth of the individual, then the idea of individual fulfillment within a framework of moral purpose must become our deepest concern, our national preoccupation, our passion, our obsession."

—John W. Gardner

"Education, once the peculiar privilege of the few, must in our best earthly estate become the valued possession of the many. It is a natural and inalienable right of human souls."

—John H. Vincent

"You should have education enough so that you won't have to look up to people; and then more education so that you will be wise enough not to look down on people."

—M. L. Bowen

13 ADULT EDUCATION
study and practice

> "Every man who rises above the common level has received two educations: the first from his teachers; the second, more personal and important, from himself."
>
> —Edward Gibbon

Adult Education as Old as Man

Only in relatively recent years has the word "education" been primarily associated with youth. Adult education reaches back to ancient times. Confucius, Isaiah, Micah, Aristotle, Plato, Jesus, virtually all the great thinkers and teachers in history, devoted their attention to developing mature minds. Indeed the great social movements that produced Western civilization were all founded on the conviction that the adult mind could learn and change.

Three Uses of Term "Adult Education"

1. *A Field of Study* — An Academic Discipline

    The first Ph.D. in Adult Education was given in 1935 by Columbia University, where Thorndike's work on adult learning was done. Since that time more than 60 universities have developed graduate programs in adult education and an increasing body of trained professionals have received advanced degrees. Research in the field, though much is still needed, has accelerated.

2. *A Field of Professional Practice* — Institutions and Agencies

    The term "adult education" refers to the entire group of organized activities carried on for adults by a wide variety of institutions for the attainment of educational objectives. It includes organized classes, study groups, lecture series, workshops, conferences, planned reading programs, guided discussions, and correspondence courses, and its professionals include all those who administer, coordinate, teach, lead or counsel in such institutional programs for adults.

3. *An Adult Activity* — A Part of Every Adult Life

    The term "adult education" also is used to describe the process by which men and women continue learning after formal youth education is completed. In this sense it includes all forms of experience — reading, listening, traveling, conversing, attending classes, participating in groups — all activities engaged in by people for the purpose of learning.

What Does Adult Education Include?

1. Perhaps the easiest way to describe "adult education" is to say that it includes all education that is *not* elementary, secondary or higher education. But even this broad description breaks down, for adult basic education is essentially elementary and secondary education for adults, and higher education may be considered adult education when adults attend, particularly as part-time evening students.

2. Adult Education includes under its umbrella such areas as

   - Lifelong Learning
   - Human Resource Development
   - Technical Education
   - Vocational Education
   - Career Education
   - Continuing Education
   - Leisure Education
   - Community Education (for adults)
   - Adult Basic Education
   - Relgious Adult Education
   - Training in Business and Industry
   - Labor Education
   - Health Education
   - Family Life Education
   - Consumer Affairs Education
   - Public Affairs Education
   - Adult Counseling
   - Recurrent Education
   - Inservice Training
   - Workplace Education

3. In the federal legislation for "Lifelong Learning" (a more recent term for "adult education"), the act states: "Lifelong learning includes, but is not limited to, adult basic education, continuing education, independent study, agricultural education, business education and labor education, occupational education and job training programs, parent education, postsecondary education, preretirement and education for older and retired people, remedial education, special education programs for groups or for individuals with special needs, also educational activities designed to upgrade occupational and professional skills, to assist business, public agencies, and other organizations in the use of innovation and research results, and to serve family needs and personal development."

further study references: 7, 157, 159, 171, 196, 264, 268,

Factors and Forces Affecting Adult Education Today

1. **Participation**. A study of participation trends in adult education from 1969-1984 was conducted by the U.S. Center for Education Statistics. Data were collected triennially on 60,000 households of persons who provided information about participation in formal part-time adult education to Census Bureau interviewers. Among the findings and conclusions:

   - The number of persons involved in adult education increased 79 percent from 1969 to 1984, while the population 17 years old and over increased 33 percent. This growth reflects a changing concept of education in which formal instruction does not stop with a high school or college degree, but continues throughout one's life.

   - Several groups were over represented in their participation patterns: whites, persons with a college education, persons living in the Western states, persons with above-median incomes, and persons working in executive, professional, or technical occupations.

   - The number of education activities or courses reported taken during a year doubled (from twenty million in 1969 to over forty million in 1984).

   - Minority participation decreased. In 1969 minorities made up 11 percent of the U.S. population but were 8 percent of participants in adult education activities. In 1984 they made up 14 percent of the U.S. population, but were still only 8 percent of participants. In contrast, in 1969 whites made up 89 percent of the population while accounting for 92 percent of participants; in 1984 they were 86 percent of the population, but still constituted 92 percent of participants.

   - Overall there was an increase in the level of participation In 1969, 10 percent of all adults were involved in adult education; by 1984, 14 percent were involved. The increases in participation occurred at all age groups, but were especially significant for the 35-54 age group and for persons 55 years old and over.

   - Adult education has become closely related to the world of work. In 1969, slightly over half of all adult education courses were taken to get a job or to advance in a job; by 1984, two-thirds of adult education was taken for job-related reasons.

   - Employer provided courses also increased. In 1984, 43 percent of the adult education courses taken for job-related reasons were provided by employers, up from 25 percent in 1969.

- Courses taken for credit decreased but those taken for renewing a license or certificate increased. In 1969, the majority of adult education courses were taken for some type of credit (i.e., for a license, degree, or certificate). By 1984, only about a third of the courses were taken for credit. However, courses taken to meet a requirement for obtaining or renewing a license or certificate in a trade or profession as required by law increased. Such remained stable from 1969 to 1975, then doubled between 1975 and 1984, from 3.2 million to 6.4 million courses. As a percent of all adult education courses, these courses accounted for 12 percent in 1975, and increased to 16 percent in 1984.

2. **Women**. Women are increasingly a larger portion of the workforce. The trend continues and is accelerating. For the last two decades women have taken two thirds of the millions of new jobs created in the information era and will continue to do so well into the millennium.

   - Women without children are more likely to work than men. Today 74 percent of men work, but 79 percent of women with no children under eighteen work. So do 67 percent of women with children.

   - Women are improving their status in professional careers--over 50 percent of students enrolled in graduate programs are women.

   - For the first time, in 1986, the number of women who intended to be doctors (25,000) exceeded those who intended to be nurses (19,000). In addition, 40 percent of managers are now women, 39 percent of attorneys are women, 31 percent of MBA graduates are women, and 13 percent of engineers are women.

   - Women provide $100 billion of the gross national product. They start up small businesses at three times the rate of men, and by the year 2000 they will own one-half of all sole proprietorships.

3. **Older adults**. The relative proportions of older adults to the population will continue to increase the call on adult education services. Programs like college for seniors, elderhostels and a host of others will dramatically increase.

   - By 1990 there were as many people over age 55 as the total number enrolled in the public schools between ages 5 and 18. Youth will comprise only 16 percent of the population by the year 2000.

   - There will be a 26 percent increase in those over the age of 75. Over 2.8 million people will be over 85. And 110,000 will be over age 100 by the year 2000.

- Currently the average lifespan is 78.6 years. On the average females live to 81 and males live to be 76.

- When the Social Security system began there were 35 workers for every retiree. Now there are three workers for every retiree and future projections show that there will be a fraction less than two workers for every retiree.

- Age of retirement will rise.

4. **College**. The traditional college age has been 18-25. Increasing numbers of adult students over that age are challenging colleges to meet the needs of adult learners.

- By 1992, one-half of all college students in the U.S. were over 25 years old. Of this, 20 percent were over 35 years of age.

- Almost all non-traditional students attend part-time as do increasing numbers of traditional college age group.

- Only 15% of the jobs of the future will require a college diploma, but over half will require postsecondary education and training.

5. **Literacy**. Estimates of the number of persons in need of literacy services range from 45 to 70 million. Fifty million adults in the U.S. do not have high school credentials and almost 2 million adults have *no* school years completed.

- The number of illiterate and functionally illiterate adults who enter this pool each year has been estimated to be about 2.3 million. The primary source of new functional illiterates is those who fail to complete high school (estimated at 1 million). Other sources include legal and illegal immigrants, refugees, and, unfortunately, some who possess high school diplomas.

- In studying adult high school non-completers, *Larry G. Martin* identified a typology of "life-style classifications" based upon their means of financial support and on their degree of socially acceptable behavior:

  —The employed group consists of three categories: skilled and unskilled workers (regulars), managers of agencies and organizations (superiors), and owners of businesses (entrepreneurs). These individuals represent a unique target population for adult literacy programs.

  —The unemployed group consists of two categories: individuals with an indirect means of financial support (suppliants) and individuals receiving public assistance (marginals). Suppliants tend to be recently unemployed persons receiving unemployment compensation, or those dependent on relatives. Marginals consist largely of the stationary poor. What all five groups have in common is socially acceptable behavior.

—Persons not characterized as having socially acceptable behavior are denominated "underclass". This underclass group mirrors the five categories above but are committed to a life-style and a belief system that is anti-social in nature. They are found in institutions that serve the criminal justice system, such as jails and prisons, and in other rehabilitative agencies, such as drug detoxication centers and halfway houses.

—Youthful non-completers (ages 16-21) are "often indifferent or hostile toward education, frustrated and embittered by their experiences in school or by chronic unemployment and lacking self-confidence and encouragement from family and peers." They require specially designed literacy programs.

—High school non-completers in the young and middle-aged adult category (ages 22-54) are often the primary target of adult literacy programs. However, lack of time is a serious constraint because of work and family responsibilities.

—High school non-completers among older learners (age 55 and older) have the lowest levels of literacy skills and the lowest level of participation in adult literacy programs.

- Federal funding for literacy education increased in the late 80's to $135 million by 1988. With increased funding came increased numbers of adults served. All service populations benefitted; however, in percentage terms, actually fewer black and white Americans were now being served compared to the need. Relatively more English as a second language (ESL) students were now served. More recent amendments to the Adult Education Act add additional requirements for serving larger numbers of institutionalized adults, increasing state and local funding match, and accountability.

- The General Educational Development (GED) diploma, designed to measure academic knowledge equivalent to that demonstrated by the top 70 percent of graduating high school seniors, is accepted by almost all employers and universities as equivalent to a standard high school diploma.

—In 1990, one-eighth of high school diplomas awarded were GED's. Ten million individuals have received GED's over the last 50 years. The GED was originally designed for veterans of World War II who dropped out of high school to fight the war.

—Most adults take the seven-and-a-half-hour test between the ages of 18 and 24. Only one percent take the test at age 55 or over.

—Of the 800,000 who took the test in 1990, 560,000 passed.

6. **Functional literacy**. At every age level and at every juncture of life the need for continuing education is evident to fully function in our society.

- An Adult Performance Level Study (conducted in 1975 with a sample of 1500 persons) funded by the Office of Education, looked at adult ability to deal with real life situations:

  —The study focused on five general areas considered necessary for adult competence: occupational knowledge, consumer economics, government and law, health, and community resources.

  —The APL report revealed the greatest area of competence to be in community resources with one-half the population in the highest functional level.

  —The study showed that Americans have more trouble with everyday problems of consumer economics than any other knowledge area. Nearly 35 million adults—almost a third of the adult population—have trouble buying life insurance, using credit, shopping wisely, and handling other facets of consumer economics.

  —One-fourth of all Americans cannot understand their rights and obligations under our system of government and law.

  —One in five adults has trouble with occupational knowledge— the basics of finding, getting, holding, and advancing in a job.

  —The health knowledge area presented problems for 21 per cent of Americans.

  —In the skills tested—reading, writing, computation, problem solving and inter-personal relations—people had the most trouble with arithmetic needed to balance a checkbook, figure the unit price of foods, and calculate interest charges on credit accounts.

  —Conclusion: 39 million Americans are unable to perform basic computations and another 30 million can barely get by!

7. **Workforce education and training**. The continuing growth of technological developments and specialized knowledge necessitates continued retraining throughout a career.

- The need for continuing education is so great that many employers routinely underwrite the cost of school for their employees. Many firms spend five percent of their payroll costs on employee training. For some employers, as much as one-third of their work force may be in school full-time or part-time at company expense. The American Society for Training and Development reports that employers currently spend about $30 billion each year for formal training and three to six times this amount on informal training, a commitment estimated to be $210 billion dollars annually. The bulk of training - as much as 60 percent - occurs at the workplace.

- Many businesses have become their own education providers. The corporate classroom is an expanding center of adult learning in the US, with the number of employees who study while on somebody's payroll at a level close to the total enrollment of all of American's four-year colleges, universities, and graduate schools combined, and the funds expended approaches the total annual expenditures of US colleges and universities. A growing number of corporate colleges are accredited and grant their own graduate degrees.

- Some 40 million Americans are currently in career transition, all requiring training for their new pursuits. This includes large numbers of "displaced workers" as industries change and "down size", as well as "displaced homemakers," older women entering the labor force.

- Technological applications require a new kind of worker, one with a broad set of basic workplace skills including information processing skills, creative thinking and problem-solving abilities, critical thinking, interpersonal skills, managing conflict, as well as reading, communication, and computation. Employers place a premium on workers with a solid foundation of basic skills that can help them learn on the job.

- As many as 30 million current workers will have to be virtually totally retrained in the next 12 years. Almost all new jobs demand a higher level of skills and require some postsecondary technical preparation training (tech prep). Access to further training for these jobs becomes quite limited with inadequate literacy skills.

- The need is so vast that it will require cooperative partnerships between and among employers, labor unions, secondary and postsecondary schools, technical institutes and proprietary schools, community colleges and universities, and will spawn entrepreneurial training organizations and consultant enterprises for the "out-sourcing" of training.

8. **Cultural diversity**. For many Americans, work is the only place where they commingle freely with those from different backgrounds. Increasing cultural diversity of the work force will require educational efforts in inter-cultural understanding and appreciation.

- Census data show that minorities (primarily African-Americans) constituted 11 percent of the U.S. civilian labor force in 1970. The proportion of minorities in the labor force rose significantly to 15.9 percent in 1980 with the addition of Hispanics in the census count: 10.2 percent for African-Americans and 5.7 percent for Hispanics. In 1987 the proportion of minorities increased 2.8 percentage points to constitute 18.7 percent of the labor force. In the year 2000 minorities are projected to constitute 21.9 percent of the labor force: 11.7 percent African-Americans and 10.2 percent Hispanics.

further study references: 47, 48, 232,

- Already, for the first time in U. S. history, current demographic profiles of the work force indicate that white males are the minority—only 46 percent. However, racial and ethnic minorities are projected to constitute 29 percent of the labor force entrants between now and the year 2000, twice the current percentage. Also, an additional 400,000 legal and illegal immigrants are projected to enter the U.S. work force annually through the balance of the century.

9. **Self-improvement.** More and more adults are searching for self-improvement, personal growth and self-actualization, studying new philosophies for life, participating in human growth and self-awareness activities.

- The increasing amount of "non-work time" has provided people with more personal hours, time to fill. A work-week of 60 hours-plus at the turn of the century is now 40, and still dropping.

- Leisure pursuits, hobbies, recreational interests, part-time secondary careers, learning programs, culture, arts, and activities of all sorts will increase.

- Lifelong learning will generate birth-to-death curriculum and delivery strategies.

> *"Absence of occupation is not rest*
> *A mind quite vacant is a mind distressed."*
> *—William Cowper*

> *"The society which scorns excellence in plumbing because plumbing is a humble activity and tolerates shoddiness in philosophy because it is an exalted activity will have neither good plumbing nor good philosophy. Neither its pipes nor its theories will hold water."*
> *—John W. Gardner*

> *"Nothing here below is profane for those who know how to see. On the contrary everything is sacred."*
> *— Teilhard de Chardin*

Institutions of Adult Education

For any agency or institution, adult education may be

- A primary end, the purpose of the agency (example: Great Books Foundation, Cooperative Extension, human growth centers, adult centers)

- An extension of the agency's purpose to an adult clientele (examples: university extension, evening colleges, public school adult education, church adult education, library outreach, museums, etc.).

- In-house for improving agency personnel performance (examples: inservice in hospitals, business, industry, government agencies, armed forces, etc.)

Who Is An Adult Educator?

It is almost as difficult to identify an adult educator as to define adult education! Many persons who are in fact adult educators (that is, their primary concern is the education of adults) do not perceive themselves as adult educators at all, because their adult education role is incidental to their primary identification as nurse, librarian, engineer, social worker, home economist, supervisor, etc.

Professional Adult Educators:

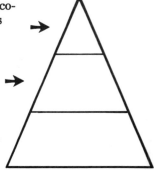

1. Full time adult educators who administer, coordinate, supervise, teach or counsel adults full-time.

2. Part-time adult educators who administer, coordinate, teach or counsel adults along with other employment. This includes thousands of "call staff" or "night school teachers."

3. Volunteers who work with adults in a variety of settings as "leaders."

Professional Organizations for Adult Education

Although membership in professional organizations primarily consists of full-time adult educators in their membership, most are open to the other two groups of adult educators as well.

1. National Organizations
   - *American Association of Adult and Continuing Education,* founded in 1982 as a result of the consolidation of the Adult Education Association of the U.S.A. (formed in 1951) and the National Association for Public Continuing and Adult Education (formed in 1952). AEA-USA itself had been a merger of the American Association of Adult Education (formed in 1926) and the Department of Adult Education of the NEA (formed in 1921). AAACE provides a professional home for all adult educators.

further study references: 78, 124, 139, 141, 161, 168, 171, 175, 300,

1) AAACE contains a variety of special units which suggest the breadth of adult education:

AAACE Commissions

Adult Basic Education
Affiliate Organizations
Business, Industry, and Labor
Community and Non-Formal Education
Continuing Professional and Higher
    Education

Military Education and Training
Professors of Adult Education
State, Provincial and Local Program
    Management

AAACE Units

Adult Psychology
Aging Education Issues
Colleges and Universities
Cooperative Extension
Correctional Institutions
Correspondence and Home Study
Distance Learning
English as a Second Language
GED Test Administrators
Health Education Issues
History and Philosophy of Adult
    Education
Human Resources Development
    and Training

International Adult Education
Minority Issues
National Adult Education Staff
    Development
New Technology
Popular Education
Religious Education
Research and Practice
Social Justice and Human Rights
Special Learning Issues
Students of Adult Education
State Directors of Adult Education
Vocational and Career Education
Women's Issues, Status and Education

- *Adult Education Research Conference* is an independent group that sponsors a yearly conference for the giving of papers on research in adult education.

- A large number of other national groups also include adult educators.
  Examples:
    —American Society of Training and Development
    —American Association of Community and Junior Colleges
    —American Association for Higher Education
    —National Community Development Association
    —Association of University Evening Colleges
    —Correctional Education Association
    —Great Books Foundation
    —National Association of County Agricultural Agents
    —National Home Demonstration Agents Association
    —National University Extension Association
    —Society of Public Health Educators
    —National Community Education Association
    —American Association of Museums
    —American Vocational Education Association
    —Religious Education Association

2. State Organizations (in most states and/or regions):

- *Example:*
  —Wisconsin Association of Adult and Continuing Education, formed by the merger of two predecessor associations: the Adult Education Association of Wisconsin, and the Adult Basic Education Association of Wisconsin.

3. Urban Adult Education Councils (in many cities)

- *Example:*
  —Milwaukee Council for Adult Learning.

The History of American Adult Education

1. **1600-1775 — Foundations and Antecedents**

- Methods: Apprenticeships; Town Meetings
- Church provided intellectual center
- Benjamin Franklin ("father of American adult education") founded Junto (1727)
- Beginnings of colleges (Harvard, 1636), libraries, museums, theaters, newspapers

2. **1775-1865 — Dominating Purpose: Diffusion of Knowledge**

- Methods: Lectures, Forums, Tracts
- Impact of dawn of age of science: curiosity
- Development of libraries and institutes providing lecture series, scientific collections, up-to-date periodicals (examples: Lowell Institute, Boston; Cooper Union, New York)
- Development of the Lyceum Movement (Josiah Holbrook) in 1826. By 1835 there were 3,000 town lyceums, over 100 county and 15 state lyceums. National system withered after 1839 but town and county lyceums continued until the Civil War and, even after the war, "Lyceum Bureaus" continued to provide speakers for groups.
- Development of voluntary associations and agencies (examples: YMCA, YWCA, National Education Association)
- Development of the Sunday School (1785), formation of the American Sunday School Union (1824).
- Formation of United States Agricultural Society (1852). By 1860 more than 840 local societies. Establishment of U.S. Department of Agriculture, and passage of the Land-Grant (Morrill) Act in 1862.

> "Americans of all ages, all conditions, and all dispositions constantly form associations. They have not only commercial and manufacturing companies, in which all take part, but associations of a thousand other kinds, religious, moral, serious, futile, general or restricted, enormous or diminutive. The Americans make associations to give entertainments, to found seminaries, to build inns, to construct churches, to diffuse books, to send missionaries to the antipodes; in this manner they found hospitals, prisons, and schools. If it is proposed to inculcate some truth or to foster some feeling by the encouragement of a great example, they form a society. Wherever at the head of some new undertaking you see the government in France, or a man of rank in England, in the United States you will be sure to find an association." —*Alexis de Tocqueville, 1831*

3. **1865-1920 — Diffusion of Organizations**

- Methods: Lectures, Meetings, Institutes, Demonstrations, Correspondence Study

- Wave after wave of immigrants swelled population from just over 30 million in 1860 to over 100 million by 1920.

- Development of the Chautauqua (John Vincent and Lewis Miller) in 1874, initially a pan-denominational normal school for Sunday School teachers, but by 1878 expanded in scope to become The Chautauqua Literary and Scientific Circle, providing a four-year program of home reading for local reading circles, a series of summer schools, a program of correspondence courses, and an extensive informal program of lectures series, conferences, concerts, plays and special interests clubs, under leadership of William Rainey Harper. Hundreds of local and regional "chautauquas" were formed, imitating the parent model.

- Correspondence courses proliferated. Literally hundreds of correspondence schools were formed by private individuals, partnerships and stock companies, mostly providing vocational offerings. When Dr. Harper became president of the University of Chicago in 1892, he established a correspondence division, and the idea spread to other universities.

- Establishment of Farmers' Institutes sponsored by state boards of agriculture. By 1899 there were institutes in almost every state. Initiation of farmers' cooperative demonstration work (Seamon A. Knapp) and refinement of demonstration method.

- Passage of Smith-Lever Act in 1914 (Cooperative Extension Service), setting up federal support (matched by state and local funds) for "county agents." By 1918 a strong cooperative extension service (also called agricultural extension) was established in every state with a county agent in virtually every county. The service, linked to the state land-grant college, was and is an enormously successful adult education system.

- Formation of the American Federation of Labor (Samuel Gompers) in 1881 and later establishment of activities in worker's education (such as Breadwinner's College and Rand School of Social Science in New York). First educational departments in labor unions were in International Ladies Garment Workers' Union, and the Amalgamated Clothing Workers' Union.

- Tremendous growth in numbers of colleges and universities, ex panded curricula, increases in size of enrollments. Graduate study and summer sessions introduced.

- Development of university extension, taking lectures and classes beyond the campus. Idea spread rapidly. By 1891, 28 states had some kind of extension work. National University Extension As sociation founded in 1915.

- Passage of Smith-Hughes Act in 1919, making federal funds available (matched by state and local) for vocational education, in agriculture, home economics, trades, industries and commerce.

- Libraries received impetus from Andrew Carnegie grants of over $41 million for building of libraries in communities.

- Development of evening schools in public elementary and secondary schools, including "Americanization" programs for immigrants, vocational courses, and opening of evening high schools.

- Formation of an incredible number of voluntary associations and agencies: women's groups, youth groups, health, welfare and recreational agencies, fraternal organizations, service clubs, parent education organizations, public affairs education agencies, intergroup education organizations (like the NAACP, Urban League, Anti-Defamation League), professional societies, economic organizations (Chamber of Commerce, Cooperatives, Credit Unions), literally hundreds of national organizations.

4. 1920-1990 — Shaping of a Field

- Methods: Classes, Courses, Conferences, Workshops, Advocacy

- Professional Development of Field

- In 1921 the Department of Immigrant Education was established in the National Education Association. It gradually broadened its scope and in 1924 changed its name to Department of Adult Education, drawing its membership from the public school field.

- In 1926 the American Association for Adult Education was founded as a national clearing house for information on adult education, conducting an annual conference, publishing a quarterly, *Adult Education Journal* (1926-51), sponsoring many studies, publishing a large library of books. It was largely financed by the Carnegie Corporation.

- In 1951 the Department of Adult Education in NEA and the American Association for Adult Education were merged to form the Adult Education Association of the USA. The merger was short-lived, for within two years the public school people broke away to form the National Association of Public School Adult Education (NAPSAE), later changing the name to National Association of Public Continuing Adult Education.

- In 1922 Columbia University offered the first college course on "adult education." In 1928 E. L. Thorndike of Columbia did his landmark study on adult learning., and the first Ph.D. degree in adult education was granted by Columbia in 1935.

further study references: 25, 71, 124, 147, 165, 172, 269, 308,

- In the 1930's federal support for adult education activities came through the Works Progress Administration (WPA), the National Youth Administration (NYA), and the Civilian Conservation Corps (CCC).

- In the 1940's the GI Bill of Rights provided educational aid so millions of veterans could obtain a college education, and spawned a variety of adult education enterprises.

- In the 1940's the National Training Laboratory, an adjunct of the National Education Association, triggered the development of wide interest in group dynamics, leadership development, and led to the personal growth and human potential movement.

- The Adult Education Act of 1966 provided funding for basic adult education programs initially begun under the Elementary and Secondary education Act. Funds have increased from $3 million in 1965 to over $134 million in 1988, leading to rapid growth in ABE programs.

- Title I of the Higher Education Act of 1965 provided funding for community service and continuing education programs conducted by institutions of higher education to encourage institutions to program particularly for urban and suburban populations.

- The Older Americans Act of 1965 provided funding for programs for older people, a portion of which is expended in support of educational programs for older people and persons who work with older people.

- A large number of other acts of recent years have had adult education components, including the Manpower Development and Training Act, Comprehensive Employment Training Act, Community Education Act, the Lifelong Learning Act, the Fund for the Improvement of Postsecondary Education, as well as such long-standing continuing federally supported programs under earlier acts, such as cooperative extension, vocational education, etc. In fact, virtually every federal department and agency has responsibility for administering some act providing funding for adult education.

- The development of the Continuing Education Unit (CEU) and its wide adoption by agencies offering courses in adult education provides the basis for a record keeping system of continuing education participation.

- Passage of the Americans With Disabilities Act of 1990 which set forth civil rights for disabled men and women with respect to employment, housing, transportation, education, and access to public services created increased demand for adult educators and adult education agencies to provide services to help disabled adults to attain and maintain the knowledge and skills required.

- There was renewed interest in literacy becoming something of "literacy movement" in the late 80's. Adult literacy became a majc issue for a variety of federal programs, including the Job Trainin Partnership Act (JTPA), vocational education, welfare reform, Jo Opportunities and Basic Skills (JOBS), family literacy, beginning wit the reauthorization of the Adult Education Act in 1988. Congress, th White House and the American public with a host of new player including governors, literacy coalitions and other national and stat associations led to passage of the National Literacy Act of 1991 whic continued provisions of the Adult Education Act, authorized stat literacy and resource centers, encouraged technology developmen assistance to literacy instructors, a functional literacy for prisoner program, and a National Center on Adult Literacy.

- The thrust of the 90's will be in workplace training, involvin secondary schools, communities, industry and business, governmer at all levels, and labor unions, finding creative ways to finance jo training including tax credits, redirecting resources to insure stat(supported vocational and technical training targeted to high-deman occupations, creating vehicles for brokering cooperation betwee industry and training institutions, targeting training for dislocate and disabled workers, and utilizing telecommunications, vide technology and television for self-paced training instruction.

> *"Perhaps the most valuable result of all education is the ability to make yourself do the thing you have to do when it has to be done, whether you like it or not."*
> —*Aldous Leonard Huxley*

> *"The inertia of deeply entrenched mental models can overwhelm even the best systematic insights."*
> — *Peter M. Senge*

> *"I know of no safe depository of the ultimate powers of society but the people themselves; and if we think them not enlightened enough to exercise their control with a wholesome discretion, the remedy is not to take it from them, but to inform their discretion by education."*
> — *Thomas Jefferson*

Some Projections on the Future of American Adult Education

1. A merging or coalition of professional associations of adult educators at the national, state and local levels.

    -   The many-voiced, often competing and frequently weak associations will gain strength and purpose in union, coalition, and cooperation to become dynamic visible spokesmen for adult education.

2. The concept of lifelong learning accepted and given a priority among the competing needs of adults.

    -   The long prevailing attitude that adult education is a frill and easily eliminated will become history.

3. Adequate funding for adult education.

    -   Ways must be found for appropriately and adequately financing adult education for *all* adults. Too much of adult education today is limited to those who can afford to pay the cost, *i.e.,*the more education you have, the more you will be able to get.

4. Adult education seen as an important and vital function in its own right in each agency, institution or organization.

    -   Historically adult education is secondary to the purposes of the agency or organization to which it is attached and thus regarded as marginal or peripheral. Now it will tend to be central.

5. More emphasis on parenthood and family life education.

    -   Single parent families, step-parents, families reared far from grandparents or other relatives, changing roles of women and men, make this area a priority for programs.

6. Increased emphasis on vocational, technical and continuing education to up-date workplace knowledge and skills.

    -   Every five years or so people require retraining, perhaps four or five times, or as many as ten to twelve times, in the course of a 40-year working life. Education is never complete.

7. Increased need for educational opportunities for adults who wish to change careers.

    -   Greater numbers of adults are electing to change careers, especially at mid-life or upon early retirement from a previous career.

8. Dramatic growth in educational programming for older adults.

    -   Greater numbers of adults in the over-65 group will demand and receive educational programming.

9. Massive increase in adult education through the mass media.

    -   Television particularly, and other mass media, will be increasingly used for adult education.

10. Increased emphasis on health education.

   - The recognition that ultimately each individual is responsible for his/her own health will lead to intense development of "patient education," "wellness," and "preventive health" programs.

11. A greater emphasis on effective training and development of volunteers.

   - Increasing numbers of volunteers, from board members to aides to leaders to committee members, in hundreds of contexts need continuing education.

12. Continued movement toward competency based adult education.

   - Adult basic education as well as vocational and technical education will be tied to competency and outcome criteria. Virtually *all* programs will be under pressure to identify the competencies the program aims to achieve.

13. Continued increase in credentialling and certification programs requiring continuing education.

   - Most certification programs will be time-limited with renewal tied to continuing education.

14. Universal acceptance of the CEU.

   - The Continuing Education Unit, already widely accepted, will continue with the addition of procedures for validation of learning.

15. The right of every adult to functional literacy.

   - Adequate funding and opportunity for adult basic education will ultimately become national policy.

16. Development of more innovative and flexible programming and delivery systems in institutions providing adult education.

   - At every level of adult education, there will be greater creativity in designing and timing programs for adults (in-plant, weekends, third shift, etc.)

17. Institutional developments to serve the self-directed learner.

   - Few institutions are yet geared to serve the needs of the self-motivated, self-directed learner who seeks resources and help to learn.

18. A system of brokering, of putting adults in contact with other adults willing to help and teach.

   - Perhaps adult counseling centers will make increased use of computerized information for making appropriate matches between adult learners and learning resources.

19. The use of Adult Education Advisory Councils at all levels, federal, state and local, cutting across program and agency lines.

   - The need for better coordination and cooperation among and between programs is imperative.

further study references: 2, 84, 115, 202, 221

20. An effective national clearing house for information relative to the education of adults.

   - The wheel is being invented too many times in too many places.

21. A clearly defined unit for adult education in the federal bureaucracy and a national policy on adult education.

   - Far too many federal agencies and departments are involved in adult education with right hands not knowing what left hands are doing.

22. Continued development of a knowledge base for adult education.

   - Research in adult learning, adult development, adult needs, adult programming, adult teaching, learning styles, etc. is much needed and especially integrative theory building.

23. A well-trained cadre of adult educators in every agency or institution.

   - Increasingly those being employed in leadership positions in adult and continuing education will be persons with master's and doctor's degrees in adult education.

24. A growing and almost unlimited variety of courses available for adults in all walks of life.

   - Virtually every organization and agency will provide learning opportunities for all ages, from young adults to senior citizens, from basic to college level, and to meet every conceivable need.

25. Expansion of continuing professional education as context for individual growth and development.

   - More emphasis on transformative learning and reflection-in-practice and professional needs in the work context and in the contexts of family and community.

26. Development and implementation of programs that foster cultural understanding.

   - The increasing diversity of society and workplace in a global world village will spur increased programs for understanding and appreciating cultural diversity.

27. Emphasis on human resource development and rapid growth of workplace education and "tech prep" programs.

   - Cooperative arrangements with community colleges, technical institutes, private vendors, labor organizations, and employers to meet the demands for growth of workplace training.

28. Greater use of educational technology.

   - Computers, CD-ROM's, interactive video disks, VCR's, telecommunications technologies, satellites, interconnections and linkages between technologies, on-line computer networking services, electronic data interchange—a new information technology industry known as the information superhighway.

THE TEACHER OF ADULT

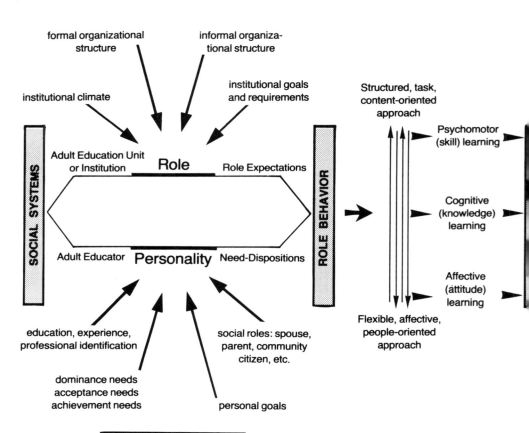

ORGANIZATIONAL FORCES

formal organizational structure

informal organizational structure

institutional goals and requirements

institutional climate

Structured, task, content-oriented approach

SOCIAL SYSTEMS

Adult Education Unit or Institution

Role

Role Expectations

ROLE BEHAVIOR

Psychomotor (skill) learning

Cognitive (knowledge) learning

Adult Educator Personality Need-Dispositions

Affective (attitude) learning

education, experience, professional identification

social roles: spouse, parent, community citizen, etc.

Flexible, affective, people-oriented approach

dominance needs acceptance needs achievement needs

personal goals

INDIVIDUAL FORCES

a model of adult education

JLT LEARNING

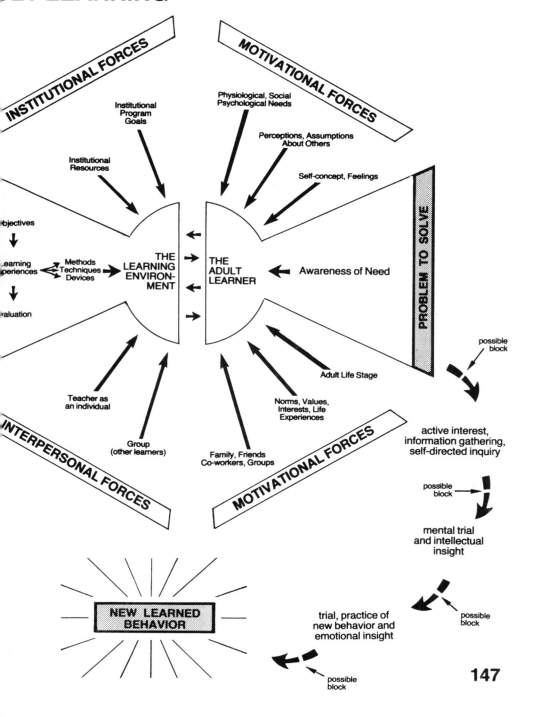

INSTITUTIONAL FORCES

MOTIVATIONAL FORCES

Institutional Program Goals

Physiological, Social Psychological Needs

Perceptions, Assumptions About Others

Institutional Resources

Self-concept, Feelings

bjectives

Methods Techniques Devices

THE LEARNING ENVIRON-MENT

THE ADULT LEARNER

Awareness of Need

PROBLEM TO SOLVE

earning periences

valuation

possible block

Teacher as an individual

Adult Life Stage

Norms, Values, Interests, Life Experiences

active interest, information gathering, self-directed inquiry

Group (other learners)

Family, Friends Co-workers, Groups

possible block

INTERPERSONAL FORCES

MOTIVATIONAL FORCES

mental trial and intellectual insight

NEW LEARNED BEHAVIOR

trial, practice of new behavior and emotional insight

possible block

possible block

147

> *"The purpose of life, after all, is to live it, to taste experience to the utmost, to reach out eagerly and without fear for newer and richer experience."*
> — *Eleanor Roosevelt*

> *"Whatever you can do, or dream you can, begin it. Boldness has genius, power and magic in it."*
> —*Johann W. von Goethe*

> *"Yesterday is already a dream, and tomorrow is only a vision; but today well-lived makes every yesterday a dream of happiness, and every tomorrow a vision of hope."*
> —*from the Sanskrit*

> *"The idea. . .that life is a vale of tears is just as false as the idea. . .that life is a place of entertainment. Life is a place of service."*
> —*Leo Tolstoi*

BIBLIOGRAPHY
references for further study

> "The true university of these days is a collection of books."
> —Thomas Carlyle

1. Allport, Gordon W. *Becoming*. New Haven, Ct: Yale University Press, 1955.

2. Anderson, Richard E. and E. K. Kasl. *The Costs and Financing of Adult Education and Training*. Lexington, KY: Heath, 1982.

3. Apps, Jerold W. *Improving Practice in Continuing Education*. San Francisco: Jossey-Bass, 1985.

4. Apps, J. W. *Higher Education in a Learning Society*. San Francisco: Jossey-Bass, 1988.

5. Apps, J. W. *The Adult Learner on Campus*. Chicago: Follett, 1981.

6. Apps, J. W. *Toward a Working Philosophy of Adult Education*. Syracuse, NY: Syracuse University Publications in Continuing Education, 1973.

7. Apps, J. W. *Study Skills for Adults Returning to School*. New York: McGraw-Hill, 1978.

8. Argyris, Chris. *Reasoning, Learning, and Action*. San Francisco: Jossey-Bass, 1982.

9. Argyris, C., R. Putnam and D. M. Smith. *Action Science: Concepts, Methods and Skills*. San Francisco: Jossey-Bass, 1985.

10. Aslanian, C. B. and H. M. Bricknell. *Americans in Transition: Life, Changes as Reasons for Learning*. New York: College Entrance Examination Board, 1980.

11. Atchley Robert C. *The Social Forces in Later Life: An Introduction to Social Gerontology*. Belmont, CA: Wadsworth Publishing Co., 1977.

12. Bard, Ray, and others. *The Trainer's Professional Development Handbook*. San Francisco: Jossey-Bass, 1987.

13. Beal, George M., Joe M. Bohlen, and J. Neil Raudabaugh. *Leadership and Dynamic Group Action*. Ames, IA: Iowa State University Press, 1962.

14. Beder, Hal. *Adult Literacy: Issues for Policy and Practice*. Malabar, FL: Krieger, 1991.

15. Beder, H. (ed). *Marketing Continuing Education*. San Francisco: Jossey-Bass, 1986.

16. Belenky, M. F., B. M. Clinchy, N. G. Godberger and J. M. Tarule. *Women's Ways of Knowing*. New York: Basic Books, 1986.

17. Bennis, Warren C., K. D. Benne and R. Chin. *The Planning of Change*. New York: Holt, Rinehart and Winston, 1985.

18. Bergevin, Paul and John McKinley. *Design for Adult Education in the Church.* Greenwich, Ct: Seabury Press, 1958.

19. Bergevin, P. and J. McKinley. *A Philosophy for Adult Education.* New York: Seabury Press, 1967.

20. Bergevin, P., D. Morris and R. M. Smith. *Adult Education Procedures: A Handbook of Tested Patterns for Effective Participation.* New York: Seabury Press, 1963.

21. Berne, Eric. *What Do You Say After You Say Hello?* New York: Grove Press, 1972.

22. Biddle, William W. and Loureide J. Biddle. *The Community Development Process.* New York: Holt, Rinehart and Winston, 1965.

23. Birren, James E. *The Psychology of Aging.* Englewood Cliffs, NJ: Prentice-Hall, 1964.

24. Bischof, Ledford J. *Adult Psychology*, second edition. New York: Harper and Row, 1976.

25. Blackburn, Donald J. *Foundations and Changing Practices in Extension.* University of Guelph, 1989.

26. Bolles, Richard. *The Three Boxes of Life.* Berkeley, CA: Ten Speed Press, 1978.

27. Boone, E. J., R. W. Shearon, E. E. White. *Serving Personal and Community Needs Through Adult Education.* San Francisco: Jossey-Bass, 1981.

28. Boshear, Walton C. and Karl G. Albrecht. *Understanding People, Models and Concepts.* LaJolla, CA: University Associates, 1977.

29. Boshier, R. *Toward a Learning Society.* Vancouver: Learning Press, 1986.

30. Bower, Sharon Anthony, and Gordon H. Bower. *Asserting Yourself: A Practical Guide for Positive Change.* Reading, MA: Addison-Wesley, 1976.

31. Boyd, Robert D. and Jerold W. Apps (eds). *Redefining the Discipline of Adult Education.* San Francisco: Jossey-Bass Publishers, 1980.

32. Boyle, Patrick G. *Planning Better Programs.* New York: McGraw-Hill, 1981.

33. Bradford, Leland P. (ed). *Group Development.* LaJolla, CA: University Associates, 1974.

34. Bradford, L. *Human Forces in Teaching and Learning.* LaJolla, CA: University Associates, 1976.

35. Brammer, Lawrence M. *The Helping Relationship: Process and Skills.* Englewood Cliffs, NJ: Prentice Hall, 1973.

36. Brockett, R. G. and R. Hiemstra. *Self-Direction in Adult Learning.* New York: Routledge and Kegan Paul, 1991.

37. Brookfield, S. D. *Developing Critical Thinkers: Challenging Adults to Explore Alternative Ways of Thinking and Acting.* San Francisco: Jossey-Bass, 1988.

38. Brookfield, Stephen D. *The Skillful Teacher.* San Francisco: Jossey-Bass, 1990.

39. Brookfield, S. D. (ed) *Self-Directed Learning: From Theory to Practice.* San Francisco: Jossey-Bass, 1985.

40. Brookfield, S. D. *Understanding and Facilitating Adult Learning: A Comprehensive Analysis of Principles and Effective Practice.* San Francisco: Jossey-Bass, 1986.

41. Brunner, Edmund, et al. *An Overview of Adult Education Research.* Washington DC: Adult Education Association of the USA, 1959.

42. Bryson, Lyman. *Adult Education.* New York: American Book Co., 1936.

43. Buhler, Charlotte and Fred Massarik, (eds). *The Course of Human Life.* New York: Springer, 1968.

44. Butler, Kathleen A. *Learning and Style in Theory and Practice.* Maynard, MA: Gabriel Systems, 1984.

45. Caffarella, Rosemary. *Program Development and Evaluation: Resource Book for Trainers.* John Wiley & Sons, 1988.

46. Candy, Philip C. *Self-Direction for Lifelong Learning.* San Francisco: Jossey-Bass, 1991.

47. Cassara, Beverly B. (ed). *Adult Education in a Multicultural Society.* New York: Routledge, 1990.

48. Cervero, Ronald M. *Effective Continuing Education for Professionals.* San Francisco: Jossey-Bass, 1988.

49. Chopra, Deepak. *Ageless Body, Timeless Mind.* New York: Harmony Books, 1993.

50. Cookson, Peter S. (ed) *Recruiting and Retaining Adult Students.* New Directions for Continuing Education. San Francisco: Jossey-Bass, 1989.

51. Craig, R.L. and L. R. Bittel (eds). *Training and Development Handbook* (2nd edition). New York: Macmillan, 1976.

52. Cross, K. Patricia. *Adults as Learners: Increasing Participation and Facilitation Learning.* San Francisco: Jossey-Bass, 1981.

53. Cross, K. P. and others. *Planning Nontraditional Programs.* San Francisco: Jossey-Bass, 1974.

54. Cross, Wilbur and Carol Florio. *You Are Never Too Old to Learn.* New York: McGraw-Hill, 1979.

55. Crystal, John and Richard Bolles. *Where Do I Go From Here With My Life?* New York: Seabury Press, 1974.

56. Curtin, Sharon. *Nobody Ever Died of Old Age.* Boston: Little Brown, 1972.

57. Daloz, Laurent A. *Effective Teaching and Mentoring.* San Francisco: Jossey-Bass, 1986.

58. Darkenwald, G. G. and S. B. Merriam. *Adult Education: Foundations of Practice.* New York: Harper and Row, 1982.

59. Davis, James A. *Great Books and Small Groups.* New York: The Free Press, 1961.

60. Davis, Larry N. and Earl McCallon. *Planning, Conducting, Evaluating Workshops.* Austin, TX: Learning Concepts, 1974.

61. DeBoer, John C. *Let's Plan: A Guide to the Planning Process for Voluntary Organizations.* Philadelphia: Pilgrim Press, 1970.

62. DeBono, E. *Lateral Thinking: Creativity Step by Step.* New York: Harper and Row, 1972.

63. Delbecq, Andre, Andrew H. VandeVen and David H. Gustafson. *Group Techniques for Program Planning, a Guide to Nominal Group and Delphi Processes.* Glenview, IL: Scott, Foresman, 1975.

64. Deshler, David (ed) *Evaluation for Program Improvement*. New Directions for Continuing Education, No. 24. San Francisco: Jossey-Bass, 1984.

65. Donaldson, Les and Edward E. Scannell. *Human Resource Development: The New Trainer's Guide*. Reading, MA: Addison-Wesley, 1978.

66. Draves, William A. *How to Teach Adults*. Manhatten, KS: Learning Resources Network, 1984.

67. Dunn, Kenneth and Rita Dunn. *Teaching Students Through Their Individual Learning Styles*. Reston, VA: Prentice-Hall, 1978.

68. Dyer, Wayne W. *Your Erroneous Zones*. New York: Funk and Wagnalls, 1976.

69. Ellis, Albert and R. A. Harper. *A New Guide to Rational Living*. North Hollywood: Wilshire Book Co., 1975.

70. Erickson, E. H. *Adulthood*. New York: Norton, 1978.

71. Evans, Rupert N. and E. L. Herr. *Foundations of Vocational Education*. Columbus: Charles E. Merrill, 1978.

72. Farlow, Helen. *Publicizing and Promoting Programs*. Glenview, IL: Scott Foresman, 1975.

73. Fellenz, R. A. and G. J. Conti. *Intelligence and Adult Learning*. Bozeman MT: Center for Adult Learning, 1990.

74. Fellenz, R. A. *Cognition and the Adult Learner*. Bozeman, MT: Center for adult Learning Research, 1988.

75. Filley, Alan C. *Interpersonal Conflict Resolution*. Glenview, IL: Scott Foresman, 1975.

76. Fingeret, Arlene and Paul Jurmo (eds). *Participatory Literacy Education*. San Francisco: Jossey-Bass, 1989.

77. Fischer, R. B., M. L. Blazey and H. T. Lipman. *Students of the Third Age. University/College Programs for Retired Adults*. New York: Macmillan, 1992.

78. Fisher, James C. and K. M. Cole. *Leadership and Management of Volunteer Programs*. San Francisco: Jossey-Bass, 1993.

79. Ford, Edward E. and Robert L. Zorn. *Why Be Lonely?* Niles, IL: Argus Communications, 1975.

80. Frankel, Viktor E. *Man's Search for Meaning*. New York: Washington Square Press, 1963.

81. Freire, Paulo. *Pedagogy of the Oppressed*. New York: Continuum, 1970.

82. Freire, P. *Education for Critical Consciousness*. New York: Seabury, 1973.

83. Fromm, Erich. *The Art of Loving*. New York: Harper and Row, 1956.

84. *Future Directions for a Learning Society*. New York: College Entrance Examinations Board, 1978.

85. Galbraith, M. (ed). *Adult Learning Methods*. Malabar, FL: Krieger, 1990.

86. Galbraith, M. (ed) *Facilitating Adult Learning*. Malabar, FL: Krieger, 1991.

87. Gardner, Howard. *Frames of Mind*. New York: Basic Books, 1983.

88. Gardner, John W. *Self-Renewal*. New York: Harper and Row, 1964.

89. Gerlach, L. P. and V. H. Hine. *People, Power, Change: Movements of Social Transformation*. New York: Bobbs-Merrill, 1970.

90. Getzels, J. W. "The Acquisition of Values in School and Society," in *The High School in a New Era*, Francis S. Chase and Harold A. Anderson (eds). Chicago: The University of Chicago Press, 1958.

91. Getzels, J. W., J. M. Lipham and R. F. Campbell. *Educational Administration as a Social Process*. New York: Harper and Row, 1968.

92. Gilligan, Carol. *In a Different Voice: Psychology Theory and Women's Development*. Cambridge: Harvard University Press, 1982.

93. Gibson, Terry and Trisha Day. *Appeals: An Extension Programming Tool*. Madison, WI: Division of Program and Staff Development, University of Wisconsin-Extension, 1976.

94. Gibson, T. and T. Day. *Strategies for Involvement*. Madison, WI: Division of Program and Staff Development, University of Wisconsin-Extension, 1976.

95. Glasser, William. *Control Theory: A New Explanation of How We Control Our Lives*. New York: Harper and Row, 1984.

96. Glasser, W. *The Quality School*. New York: Harper and Row, 1990.

97. Glasser, W. *Reality Therapy*. New York: Harper and Row, 1965.

98. Gould, S. B. and K. P. Cross (eds) *Explorations in Non-Traditional Study*. San Francisco: Jossey-Bass, 1972.

99. Gordon, Thomas. *Group Centered Leadership*. Boston: Houghton Mifflin, 1955.

100. Gordon, T. *T.E.T. Teacher Effectiveness Training*. New York: David McKay Co., 1974.

101. Gould, Roger. *Transformations: Growth and Change in Adult Life*. New York: Simon and Schuster, 1978.

102. Grattan, C. Hartley. *American Ideas About Adult Education, 1710-1951*. New York: Teachers College, Columbia University, 1959.

103. Grattan, C. H. *In Quest of Knowledge*. New York: Association Press, 1955.

104. Greenblatt, C. S. *Designing Games and Simulations*. Newbury Park, CA: Sage, 1988.

105. Gregorc, Anthony. *An Adult's Guide to Style*. Maynard, MA: Gabriel Systems, 1982.

106. Gross, Ronald. *The Lifelong Learner*. New York: Simon and Schuster, 1977.

107. Gross, R. (ed). *Invitation to Lifelong Learning*. Chicago: Follett, 1992.

108. Gross, R., B. Gross and S. Seidman. *The New Old: Struggling for Decent Aging*. Garden City, NY: Anchor Press, 1978.

109. Grotelueschen, Arden D. and others. *An Evaluation Planner*. Urbana, IL: Office for the Study of Continuing Professional Education, University of Illinois at Urbana-Champaign, 1974.

110. Grotelueschen, A. D., D. G. Gooler and A. B. Knox. *Evaluation in Adult Basic Education: How and Why*. Urbana, IL: College of Education, 1976.

111. Guba, Egon G. and Yvonna Lincoln. *Effective Evaluation*. San Francisco: Jossey-Bass, 1988.

112. Hagberg, Janet, and Richard Leider. *The Inventurers: Excursions in Life and Career Renewal*. Menlo Park, CA: Addison-Wesley, 1978.

113. Hale, Noreen. *The Older Worker*. San Francisco: Jossey-Bass, 1976.

114. Hancock, E. *The Girl Within*. New York: Fawcett Columbine, 1989.

115. Harrington, Fred Harvey. *The Future of Adult Education*. San Francisco, CA Jossey-Bass, 1977.

116. Harris, Thomas A. *I'm OK, You're OK*. New York: Harper and Row, 1967.

117. Havelock, Ronald G. *A Change Agent's Guide to Innovation in Education*. Englewood Cliffs, NJ: Educational Technology Publications, 1973.

118. Havelock, R. and M. Havelock. *Training for Change Agents*. Ann Arbor, MI Institute for Social Research, 1973.

119. Havighurst, Robert J. *Developmental Tasks and Education*. New York McKay, 1972 (originally published 1952).

120. Hayslip, B. and P. Panek. *Adult Development and Aging*. New York: Harper and Row, 1989.

121. Heerman, Barry (ed). *Personal Computers and the Adult Learner*. San Francisco: Jossey-Bass, 1986.

122. Herrmann, Ned. *The Creative Brain*. Lake Lure, NC: Brain Books, 1988.

123. Hereford, Carl F. *Changing Parental Attitudes Through Group Discussion* Austin, TX: University of Texas Press, 1963.

124. Hiemstra, Roger, *Lifelong Learning*. Lincoln, NB: Professional Educators Publications, 1976.

125. Hiemstra, R. and R. Sisco. *Individualizing Instruction: Making Learning Personal, Empowering and Successful*. San Francisco: Josey-Bass, 1990.

126. Horton, Aimee Isgrig. *The Highlander Folk School: A History of Its Major Programs*. Brooklyn, NY: Carlson, 1989.

127. Horton, Myles. *The Long Hall*. New York: Doubleday, 1989.

128. Houle, Cyril O. *Continuing Learning in the Professions*. San Francisco: Jossey Bass, 1980.

129. Houle, C. O. *The Design of Education*. San Francisco: Jossey-Bass Publishers 1976.

130. Houle, C. O. *The Inquiring Mind*. Madison, WI: University of Wisconsin Press, 1961.

131. Houle, C. O. *The Effective Board*. New York: Association Press, 1960.

132. Houle, C. O. *Patterns of Learning: New Perspectives on Life Span Education* San Francisco: Jossey-Bass, 1984.

133. Houle, C. O. *The Literature of Adult Education: A Bibliographic Essay*. San Francisco: Jossey-Bass, 1992.

134. Hudson, Frederic. *The Adult Years*. San Francisco: Jossey-Bass, 1991.

136. Hultsch, David and F. Deutsch. *Adult Development and Aging*. New York McGraw-Hill, 1981.

137. Hunsaker, Philip L., Douglas J. Mickelson, and Len Sperry. *You Can Make It Happen*. Reading, MA: Addison-Wesley, 1977.

138. Hyyck, Margaret H. and W. J. Hoyer. *Adult Development and Aging* Belmont, CA: Wadsworth, 1982.

139. Ilsley, Paul J. *Enhancing the Volunteer Experience*. San Francisco: Jossey-Bass, 1990.

140. Ilsley, P. J. (ed). *Improving Conference Designs and Outcomes.* San Francisco: Jossey-Bass, 1985.

141. Ilsley, P. J. and J. A. Niemi. *Recruiting and Training Volunteers.* New York: McGraw-Hill, 1981.

142. Ingalls, John D. *A Trainer's Guide to Andragogy: Its Concepts, Experience and Application.* Revised Edition. Washington, D.C.: U.S. Department of Health, Education and Welfare, 1973.

143. James, Muriel and Dorothy Jongeward. *Born To Win.* Menlo Park, CA: Addison-Wesley, 1971.

144. Jarvis, Peter. *Adult and Continuing Education: Theory and Practice.* London: Croom Helm, 1983.

145. Jarvis, P. *Adult Learning in the Social Context.* New York: Croom Helm, 1987.

146. Jarvis, P. *The Sociology of Adult and Continuing Education.* London: Croom Helm, 1985.

147. Jarvis, P. *Twentieth Century Thinkers in Adult Education.* London: Routledge, 1987.

148. Jensen, Gale, et al. (eds) *Adult Education: Outlines of an Emerging Field of University Study.* Washington, D.C.: Adult Education Association of USA, 1964.

150. Johnson, David W. and Robert T. Johnson. *Leading the Cooperative School.* Edina, MN: Interaction Book Co., 1989.

151. Johnstone, John W.C. and Ramon J. Rivera. *Volunteers for Learning: A Study of the Educational Pursuits of American Adults.* Chicago, IL: Aldine Publishing Co., 1965.

152. Jones, K. *Designing Your Own Simulations.* New York: Methuen, 1985.

153. Jones, K. *Interactive Learning Events: A Guide for Facilitators.* New York: Nichols, 1988.

154. Josselson, Ruthellen. *Finding Herself.* San Francisco: Jossey-Bass, 1987.

155. Jourard, Sidney. *The Transparent Self.* New York: D. Van Nostrand, 1964.

156. Joyce, Bruce. *Models of Teaching.* Englewood Cliffs: Prentice-Hall, 1986.

157. Kallen, Horace M. *Philosophical Issues in Adult Education.* Springfield, IL: Charles C. Thomas, 1962.

158. Kegen, R. *The Evolving Self: Problems and Processes in Human Development.* Cambridge: Harvard University Press, 1982.

159. Kempfer, Homer. *Adult Education.* New York: McGraw-Hill, 1955.

160. Kennedy, Carroll. *Human Development: Adult Years and Aging.* New York: Macmillan, 1978.

161. Kidd, J. Roby. *How Adults Learn,* Revised. New York: Association Press, 1973.

162. Kimmel, Douglas C. *Adulthood and Aging.* New York: John Wiley and Sons, 1974.

163. Kirn, Arthur G. and Marie O'Donahoe Kirn. *Life Work Planning,* Fourth Edition. New York: McGraw-Hill, 1978.

164. Klevins, Chester (ed). *Materials and Methods in Continuing Education.* Canoga Park, CA: Klevens Publications, 1982.

165. Knowles, Malcolm S. *The Adult Education Movement in the United States.* New York: Krieger Publishing Co., 1977.

166. Knowles, M. S. and associates. *Andragogy in Action: Applying Modern Principles of Adult Learning.* San Francisco: Jossey-Bass, 1984.

167. Knowles, M. S. *The Adult Learner: A Neglected Species.* (3rd ed) Houston: Gulf, 1984.

168. Knowles, M. S. *The Modern Practice of Adult Education: Andragogy versus Pedagogy.* New York: Cambridge Books, 1980.

169. Knowles, M. S. *Self-Directed Learning, A Guide for Learners and Teachers.* New York: Association Press, 1975.

170. Knowles, M. S. *Using Learning Contracts: Practical Approaches to Individualizing and Structuring Learning.* San Francisco: Jossey-Bass, 1986.

171. Knowles, M. S. (ed). *Handbook of Adult Education in the United States.* Chicago: Adult Education Association, 1960.

172. Knowles, M. S. *The Making of an Adult Educator.* San Francisco: Jossey-Bass, 1989.

173. Knox, Alan B. *Adult Development and Learning.* San Francisco: Jossey-Bass, 1977.

174. Knox, A. B. and associates. *Developing, Administering, and Evaluating in Adult Education.* San Francisco: Jossey-Bass, 1980.

175. Knox, A. B. *Enhancing Proficiencies of Continuing Educators.* San Francisco: Jossey-Bass Publishers, 1979.

176. Knox, A. B. *Helping Adults Learn: A Guide to Planning, Implementing and Conducting Programs.* San Francisco: Jossey-Bass, 1986.

177. Kohlberg, Lawrence. *The Philosophy of Moral Development.* San Francisco: Harper and Row, 1981.

178. Kolb, David A. *Experiential Learnings.* Englewood Cliffs: Prentice-Hall, 1984

179. Kozol, J. *Illiterate America.* New York: Doubleday, 1985.

180. Kreitlow, Burton W. and associates. *Examining Controversies in Adult Education.* San Francisco: Jossey-Bass, 1981.

181. Krup, Judy. *Adult Development: Implications for Staff Development.* Mancester, CT: Judy Arin-Krup, 1981.

182. Kubler-Ross, Elisabeth. *On Death and Dying.* New York: Macmillan, 1969.

183. Kuhlen, Raymond G. (ed). *Psychological Backgrounds of Adult Education.* Boston: Center for the Study of Liberal Education for Adults, 1963.

184. Kuhn, Thomas. *The Structure of Scientific Revolutions.* Chicago: University of Chicago, 1972.

185. Lakein, Alan. *How to Get Control of Your Time and Your Life.* New York: Wyden, 1973.

186. Laird, D. *Approaches to Training and Development.* Reading, MA: Addison-Wesley, 1978.

187. Lanning, Frank W. and Wesley A. Many (eds). *Basic Education for the Disadvantaged Adult: Theory and Practice.* Boston: Houghton Mifflin, 1966.

188. Lauffer, Armand. *The Practice of Continuing Education in the Human Services.* New York: McGraw-Hill, 1977.

89. Lawler, P. *The Keys to Adult Learning: Theory and Practical Strategies.* Philadelphia: Research for Better Schools, 1991.

90. Lenz, E. *The Art of Teaching Adults.* New York: Holt, Rinehart and Winston, 1982.

91. LeShan, Eda J. *The Wonderful Crisis of Middle Age: Some Personal Reflections.* New York: David A.McKay, 1973.

92. Levinson, Daniel J. and others. *The Seasons of a Man's Life.* New York: Alfred A. Knopf,1978.

93. Lewis, Linda H. (ed) *Experiential and Simulation Techniques for Teaching Adults.* San Francisco: Jossey-Bass, 1986.

94. Leypoldt, Martha M. *40 Ways to Teach in Groups.* Valley Forge, PA: The Judson Press,1967.

95. *Lifelong Learning During Adulthood: An Agenda for Research.* Future Directions for a Learning Society. Advisory Panel on Research Needs in Lifelong Learning during Adulthood. New York: College Entrance Examination Board, 1978.

96. Lindeman, Edward C. *The Meaning of Adult Education.* Montreal: Harvest House, 1961. (originally published 1926).

97. Lippitt, Gordon L. *Visualizing Change: Model Building and the Change Process.* LaJolla, CA: University Associates, 1973.

98. Liveright, A. A. *Strategies of Leadership in Conducting Adult Education Programs.* New York: Harper and Brothers, 1959.

99. Loeser, Herta. *Women, Work and Volunteerism.* Boston: Beacon Press, 1974.

00. Loevinger, Jane. *Ego Development: Conceptions and Theories.* San Francisco: Jossey-Bass, 1976.

01. London, Jack, Robert Wenkert and Warren O. Hagstrom. *Adult Education and Social Class.* Berkeley, CA: University of California, 1963.

02. Long, Huey B. *Adult and Continuing Education: Responding to Change.* New York: Teachers College Press, 1983.

03. Long, H. B. and R. Hiemstra. *Changing Approaches to Studying Adult Education.* San Francisco: Jossey-Bass, 1980.

04. Long, H. B. *Adult Learning: Research and Practice.* New York: Cambridge Books, 1983.

05. Lorge, Irving and others. *Adult Learning.* Washington, DC: Adult Education Association, 1965.

06. Lorge, Irving, Howard Y. McCluskey, Gale E. Jensen and Wilbur C. Hallenbeck.*Psychology of Adults: Adult Education Theory and Method.* Washington, DC: Adult Education Association of USA, 1963.

07. Loring, Rosalind K. and Herbert A. Otto. *New Life Options: The Working Woman's Resource Book.* New York: McGraw-Hill, 1976.

08. Loughary, John W. and Theresa M. Ripley. *Helping Others Help Themselves: A Guide to Counseling Skills.* New York: McGraw-Hill, 1979.

09. Loughary, J. W. and B. Hopson. *Producing Workshops, Seminars, Short Courses.* New York: Cambridge, 1977.

210. Lovell, R. B. *Adult Learning.* London: Croom Helm, 1980.

211. Lumsden, D. Barry. *The Older Adult as Learner.* New York: McGraw-Hill, 1985.

157

212. Mager, Robert F. *Developing Attitude Toward Learning*. Palo Alto, CA Fearon, 1968.

213. Mager, R. F. *Measuring Instructional Intent*. Belmont, CA: Fearon Pitman Publishers, 1973.

214. Mager, R. F. *Preparing Instructional Objectives*, second edition. Belmont, CA Fearon Publishers, 1975.

215. Mager, R. F. and K. M. Beach, Jr. *Developing Vocational Instruction*. Palo Alto, CA: Fearon Publishers, 1967.

216. Maltz, Maxwell. *Psychocybernetic Principles for Creative Living*. New York Books, 1974.

217. Marsick, V. *Learning in the Workplace*. London: Croom Helm, 1987.

218. Maslow, Abraham H. *Motivation and Personality*. New York: Harper and Row 1970.

219. Maslow, A. H. *Toward a Psychology of Being*. New York: D. Van Nostrand 1961.

220. Massey, Morris. *The People Puzzle*. Reston, VA: Reston Publishing Company 1979.

221. Matkin, Gary W. *Effective Budgeting in Continuing Education*. San Francisco: Jossey-Bass, 1985.

222. Maultsby, Maxie C. and Allie Hendricks. *You and Your Emotions*. Lexington KY: University of Kentucky Medical Center, 1974.

223. May, Rollo. *The Courage to Create*. New York: Bantam Books, 1975.

224. May, R. *Love and Will*. New York: W. W. Norton and Co., 1969.

225. McCarthy, Bernice. *The 4 MAT System: Teaching to Learning Styles* Barrington, IL: Excel, 1980.

226. McCoy, Vivian Rogers, Carol Nalbandian and Colleen Ryan. *CREATE: A New Model for Career Change Trainer's Manual*. Lawrence, KS: Adult Life Resource Center, University of Kansas,1979.

227. McCoy, Vivian Rogers, Colleen Ryan and James W. Lichtenberg. *The Adult Life Cycle: Training Manual and Reader*. Lawrence, KS: Adult Life Resource Center, University of Kansas,1978.

228. McKeachie, Wilbert J. (ed). *Learning, Cognition, and College Teaching*. San Francisco: Jossey-Bass, 1980.

229. McKenzie, Leon. *Adult Religious Education: The 20th Century Challenge*. W. Mystic, CT: Twenty-Third Publications, 1975.

230. McLagan, Patricia A. *Helping Others Learn, Designing Programs for Adults*. Reading, MA: Addison-Wesley, 1978.

231. Mee, G. *Organization for Adult Education*. New York: Longman, 1980.

232. Merriam, Sharan B. Merriam and P. M. Cunningham. *Handbook of Adult and Continuing Education*. San Francisco: Jossey-Bass, 1989.

233. Merriam, S. B. and R. S. Caffarella. *Learning in Adulthood*. San Francisco: Jossey-Bass, 1991.

234. Merriam, S. B. *Themes of Adulthood Through Literature*. New York: Teachers College Press, 1983.

235. Merriam, S. B. and M. C. Clark. *Lifelines: Patterns of Work, Love and Learning in Adulthood.* San Francisco: Jossey-Bass, 1991.

236. Mezirow, Jack. *Transformative Dimensions of Adult Learning.* San Francisco: Jossey-Bass, 1991.

238. Mezirow, J. and associates. *Fostering Critical Reflection in Adulthood: A Guide to Transformative and Emancipatory Learning.* San Francisco: Jossey-Bass, 1990.

239. Mezirow, J. *Education for Perspective Transformation: Women's Reentry Programs in Community Colleges.* New York: Center for Adult Education, Teacher's College, 1978.

240. Mezirow, J., A. Knox and G. Darkenwald. *Last Gamble on Education: Dynamics of Adult Basic Education.* Washington: Adult Education Association of USA, 1975.

241. Miller, Harry L. *Teaching and Learning in Adult Education.* New York: Macmillan, 1964.

242. Miller, H. L. (ed). *Education for the Disadvantaged.* New York: The Free Press, 1967.

243. Miller, J. B. *Toward a New Psychology of Women* (2nd ed). Boston: Beacon Press, 1986.

244. Miles, Matthew B. *Learning to Work in Groups.* New York: Teachers College, Columbia University, 1959.

245. Morgan, Barton, Glen E. Holmes and Clarence E. Bundy. *Methods in Adult Education.* Danville, IL: The Interstate, 1963.

246. Moustakas, Clark E. *Loneliness and Love.* Englewood Cliffs, NJ: Prentice-Hall, 1972.

247. Mouton, J. S. and R. R. Blake. *Synergogy: A New Strategy for Education, Training and Development.* San Francisco: Jossey-Bass, 1984.

248. Munson, L. S. *How to Conduct Training Seminars.* New York: McGraw-Hill, 1984.

249. Murphy, Gardner. *Human Potentialities.* New York: Basic Books, 1958.

250. Nadler, Leonard (ed). *The Handbook of Human Resource Development.* New York: Wiley, 1984.

251. Nadler, L. and Z. Nadler. *The Comprehensive Guide to Successful Conferences and Meetings.* San Francisco: Jossey-Bass, 1988.

252. Naylor, Harriet H. *Leadership for Volunteering.* Dryden, NY: Dryden Associates, 1976.

253. Naisbitt, John and P. Aburdene. *Megatrends 2000.* New York: William Morrow, 1990.

254. Neugarten, Bernice, (ed). *Middle Age and Aging.* Chicago: University of Chicago Press, 1966.

255. Northcutt, Norvell. *Adult Functional Competency.* Austin: Industrial and Business Training Bureau, University of Texas, 1975.

256. O'Neill, Nena and George O'Neill. *Shifting Gears: Finding Security in a Changing World.* New York: M. Evans and Co., 1974.

257. Overstreet, Harry O. *The Mature Mind.* New York: W. W. Norton, 1949.

258. Patterson, R. W. K. *Values, Education, and the Adult.* Boston: Routledge and Kegan Paul, 1979.

159

259. Penland, Patrick R. *Self-Planned Learning in America.* Pittsburgh: Book Center, University of Pittsburgh, 1977.

260. Peters, John, Peter Jarvis and associates. *Adult Education: Evolution and Achievement in a Developing Field of Study.* San Francisco: Jossey-Bass, 1991.

261. Peterson, David A. *Facilitating Education for Older Learners.* San Francisco: Jossey-Bass, 1983.

262. Peterson, Richard E. and associates. *Lifelong Learning in America.* San Francisco: Jossey-Bass, 1979.

263. Popham, W. James, *Educational Evaluation.* Englewood Cliffs, NJ: Prentice-Hall, 1975.

264. Powell, John W. *Learning Comes of Age.* New York: Association Press, 1956.

265. Pressey, Sidney L. and Raymond G. Kuhlen. *Psychological Development Through the Life Span.* New York: Harper, 1957.

266. Progoff, Ira. *Depth Psychology and Modern Man.* New York: McGraw-Hill, 1959.

267. Raths, Louis E., Merrill Harman and Sidney B. Simon. *Values and Teaching: Working with Values in the Classroom.* Columbus, OH: Charles E.Merrill Publishing Co.,1966.

268. Rauch, David B. (ed). *Priorities in Adult Education.* New York: The Macmillan Company,1972.

269. Roberts, Roy W. *Vocational and Practical Arts Education: History, Development and Principles.* New York: Harper and Row, 1965.

270. Robinson, Russell D. *An Introduction to Dynamics of Group Leadership.* Milwaukee,WI:Omnibook Co., 1989.

271. Robinson, R. D. *Teaching the Scriptures: A Study Guide for Bible Students and Teachers.* Milwaukee, WI: Bible Study Press, 1993.

272. Rogers, Carl. *On Becoming a Person.* Boston: Houghton-Mifflin, 1961.

273. Rokeach, Milton. *The Open and Closed Mind.* New York: Basic Books, 1960.

274. Rosenthal, Robert and Lenore Jacobson. *Pygmalion in the Classroom.* New York: Holt, Rinehart and Winston, 1968.

275. Ross-Gordon, Jovita M., Larry G. Martin, and Diane Buck Briscoe (eds). *Serving Culturally Diverse Populations.* New Directions for Adult and Continuing Education. San Francisco: Jossey-Bass, 1990.

276. Saint, Avice. *Learning at Work: Human Resources and Organizational Development.* Chicago: Nelson-Hall Company, 1974.

277. Samples, Bob and Bob Wohlford. *The Metaphoric Mind: A Celebration of Creative Consciousness.* Menlo Park, CA: Addison-Wesley, 1975.

278. Sanders, H. C. and others. *The Cooperative Extension Service.* Englewood Cliffs, NJ: Prentice-Hall, 1966.

279. Satir, Virginia. *Peoplemaking.* Palo Alto, CA: Science and Behavior Books, 1972.

280. Satir, V. *Your Many Faces.* Millbrae, CA: Celestial Arts, 1978.

281. Schindler-Raiman, Eva and Ronald Lippitt. *The Volunteer Community: Creative Use of Human Resources.* Washington DC: NTL Learning Resources Corporation, 1975.

282. Schlossberg, Nancy K. and Alan D. Entine. *Counseling Adults*. Monterey, CA: Brooks/Cole Publishing Co., 1977.

283. Schon, D. A. *The Reflective Practitioner: How Professionals Think in Action*. New York: Basic Books, 1983.

284. Schon, D. A. *Educating the Reflective Practitioner*. San Francisco: Jossey-Bass, 1987.

285. Schultz, R. and R. B. Ewen. *Adult Development and Aging*. New York: Macmillan, 1988.

286. Seaman, Donald F. *Working Effectively with Task-oriented Groups*. New York: McGraw-Hill, 1981.

287. Seaman, D. F. and R. A. Fellenz. *Effective Strategies for Teaching Adults*. Columbus: Merrill, 1988.

288. Selye, Hans. *Stress Without Distress*. Philadelphia: J. B. Lippincott, 1974.

289. Senge, Peter M. *The Fifth Discipline: The Art and Practice of the Learning Organization*. New York: Doubleday, 1990.

290. Shaw, M. E. and others. *Role Playing: A Practical Manual for Group Facilitators*. San Diego: University Associates, 1982.

291. Shaw, Nathan C. (ed). *Administration of Continuing Education*. Washington, DC: National Association for Public School Adult Education, 1969.

292. Sheey, Gail. *Passages: Predictable Crises of Adult Life*. New York: Hart Publishing Co., 1972.

293. Sherron, Ronald H. and Dan Barry Lumsden (eds). *Introduction to Educational Gerontology* (2nd edition) New York: Hemisphere Publishers, 1985.

294. Shor, I. and P. Freire. *A Pedagogy for Liberation*. South Hadley, MA: Bergin and Garvey, 1982.

295. Simerly, Robert G. *Planning and Marketing Conferences and Workshops*. San Francisco: Jossey-Bass, 1990.

296. Simerly, R. G. and associates. *Handbook of Marketing for Continuing Education*. San Francisco: Jossey-Bass, 1989.

297. Sinetar, Marsha. *Developing a 21st Century Mind*. New York: Ballatine Books, 1991.

298. Simon, Sidney B. and others. *Values Clarification*. New York: Hart Publishing Co., 1972.

299. Smith, Edwin H. *Literacy Education for Adolescents and Adults*. San Francisco: Boyd and Fraser, 1970.

300. Smith, Robert M., George Aker and J. R. Kidd. *Handbook of Adult Education*. New York: The Macmillan Company, 1970.

301. Smith, R. M. *Learning How to Learn: Applied Learning Theory for Adults*. San Francisco: Jossey-Bass, 1983.

302. Smith, R. M. and associates. *Learning to Learn Across the Lifespan*. San Francisco: Jossey-Bass, 1990.

303. Sork, Thomas J. (ed). *Designing and Implementing Effective Workshops*. San Francisco: Jossey-Bass, 1984.

304. Stanford, Gene and Albert E. Roark. *Human Interaction in Education*. Boston: Allyn and Baccon, 1974.

305. Stenzel, Anne K. and Helen Feeney. *Learning by the Case Method: Practice Approaches for Community Leaders.* New York: The Seabury Press, 1970.

306. Stenzel, A. K. and H. Feeney. *Volunteer Training and Development: Manual for Community Groups.* New York: The Seabury Press, 1968.

307. Stewart, David. *Adult Learning in America: Eduard Lindeman.* Malabar, Fl. Robert E. Krieger Publishing Co., 1987.

308. Strong, Merle E. and Carl J. Schaefer, *Introduction to Trade, Industrial an Technical Education.* Columbus, OH: Charles E. Merrill, 1975.

309. Strother, G. B. and J. P. Klus. *Administration of Continuing Education* Belmont, CA: Wadsworth, 1983.

310. Stubblefield, Harold. *Towards a History of Adult Education in America* Dover, NH: Croom HJelm, 1988.

311. Tennant, M. *Psychology and Adult Learning.* London: Routledge, 1988.

312. Terkel, Studs. *Working.* New York: Pantheon, 1972.

313. This, Leslie E. *The Small Meeting Planner.* Houston: Gulf, 1979.

314. Thompson, John F. *Foundations of Vocational Education: Social an Philosophical Concepts.* Englewood Cliffs, NJ: Prentice-Hall, 1973.

315. Toffler, Alvin. *Future Shock.* New York: Random House, 1970.

316. Toffler, A. *The Third Wave.* New York: Bantam Books, 1980.

317. Totten, W. Fred and Frank J. Manley. *The Community School: Basi Concepts, Function and Organization.* Galien, MI: Allied Education Council 1969.

318. Tough, Allen. *The Adult's Learning Projects: A Fresh Approach to Theory an Practice in Adult Learning.* Toronto: Ontario Institute for Studies in Education, 1971.

319. Tough, A. *Intentional Changes: A Fresh Approach to Helping People Change* Chicago: Follett, 1982.

320. Troll, Lillian E. *Early and Middle Adulthood.* Monterey, CA: Brooks/Cole Publishing Co., 1975.

321. Turner, Jeffrey S. and Donald B. Helms. *Life Span Development.* Philadelphia W. B. Saunders Co., 1979.

322. Tyler, L. E. *Thinking Creatively: A New Approach to Psychology an Individual Lives.* San Francisco: Jossey-Bass, 1983.

323. Tyler, Ralph W. *Basic Principles of Curriculum and Instruction.* Chicago University of Chicago Press, 1957.

324. Vaillant, George E. *Adaptation to Life: How the Best and the Brightest Came of Age.* Boston: Little, Brown and Company, 1977.

325. Van Ments, M. *The Effective Use of Role Play: A Handbook for Teachers and Trainers* (2nd ed). New York: Nichols, 1989.

326. Verduin, John R. Jr., Harry G. Miller and Charles E. Greer. *Adults Teaching Adults.* Austin, TX: Learning Concepts, 1977.

327. Verduin, J. R. and T. A. Clark. *Distance Education: The Foundations of Effective Practice.* San Francisco: Jossey-Bass, 1991.

328. Vermilye, Dychnan W. (ed). *Lifelong Learners--A New Clientele for Higher Learning.* San Francisco: Jossey-Bass, 1974.

329. Verner, Coolie. *Conceptual Scheme for the Identification and Classification of Processes of Adult Education.* Washington, DC: Adult Education Association, 1962.

330. Verner, C. and A. Boothe. *Adult Education.* Washington DC: Center for Applied Research in Education, 1964.

331. Verner, Coolie and Catherine V. Davison *Psychological Factors in Adult Learning and Instruction.* Tallahassee, Fl,: Florida State University, 1971.

332. Vogel, Linda J. *Teaching and Learning in Communities of Faith: Empowering Adults Through Religious Education.* San Francisco: Jossey-Bass, 1991.

333. Wenrich, R. C., J. W. Wenrich and J. D. Galloway. *Administration of Vocational Education.* Homewood, IL: American Technical Publishing, 1988.

334. Weinberg, George. *Self Creation.* New York: St. Martin's Press, 1978.

335. Willis, Sherry L. and Samuel S. Dubin (eds). *Maintaining Professional Competence.* San Francisco: Jossey-Bass, 1980.

336. Wilson, Marlene. *The Effective Management of Volunteer Programs.* Boulder, CO: Volunteer Management Associates, 1976.

337. Wlodkowski, Raymond J. *Enhancing Adult Motivation to Learn.* San Francisco: Jossey-Bass, 1985.

338. Young, R. E. (ed) *Fostering Critical Thinking.* San Francisco: Jossey-Bass, 1980.

> *"Each phase of life requires a different kind of learning, and at the adult level it means closing the gap between school and work and creating a seamless and universal system of lifelong learning opportunities."*
> — *Richard W. Riley, Secretary of Education, 1993*

Russell D. Robinson

Russell D. Robinson is professor of adult education in the Department of Administrative Leadership at the University of Wisconsin-Milwaukee. A native of Wisconsin, he joined the UWM faculty in 1963. He earned his B.S. (1950), M.S. (1961) and Ph.D. (1963) degrees at the University of Wisconsin, Madison. Prior to coming to Milwaukee, Dr. Robinson was for ten years with University Extension as youth agent for Waukesha County, primarily involved in leadership development. His youth leadership work won him national recognition and a three year fellowship in the National Extension Center for Advanced Study.

For his first five years at UWM he was on a joint appointment with University Extension, first as a state youth development specialist and later as an urban community programs specialist. He resigned his half-time Extension assignment in 1968 and since then has devoted full time to the adult education graduate program which he initiated and developed at UWM. Since the program began in 1966, more than 750 have been awarded master's degrees, and 15 have completed Ph.D. degrees under his direction. From 1978 to 1982 he served as chairperson of the Department of Administrative Leadership. Since 1990, he has served as director of the Institute for the Development of Effective Administrative Leadership (IDEAL).

Dr. Robinson has been active in professional adult education groups, having served as a member of the Executive Committee of the Adult Education Association of the USA, chairman of the National Council of Affiliate Adult Education Organizations, chairman of the Commission on Adult Education Research for the United States and Canada, secretary-treasurer of the Commission of Professors of Adult Education, president of the Wisconsin Association of Adult and Continuing Education, chairman of the Wisconsin Adult Educator Lyceum, and president of the Milwaukee Council for Adult Learning. In 1974 he was the recipient of the Distinguished Service Award given by the Milwaukee Council for "outstanding leadership, inspired teaching, and service to the community in adult education." In 1985 he received the WAACE "Adult Educator of the Year" award for leadership, and the same year received a national leadership award from the AAACE for chairing the national conference. In 1991 he received the WAACE President's Award "in recognition of 33 years of superb leadership and commitment to excellence in Wisconsin adult and continuing education."

He is a practitioner as well as professor of adult education, regularly teaching non-credit adult courses and in-service workshops in leadership, group dynamics, planned change, human relations, adult learning, and program development to groups of adult educators including administrators, teachers, clergy, nurses, and others. In 1977 the Milwaukee Council awarded him its Recognition of Achievement Award for his conducting more than 40 workshops for nurses.

He participates in a variety of community and state boards and committees. His service has included the Board of Future Milwaukee, the Milwaukee Inter-Institutional Committee for Higher Education Title I Programs, the Continuing Education Committee of the Mental Health Association in Milwaukee County, the Milwaukee Advisory Committee on Basic Adult Education, the International Cooperative Training Center Advisory Committee, the Wisconsin Recreation Leaders' Laboratory, the Advisory Committee of the Planned Parenthood Center for Training in Family Planning, and others.

For five years he directed Project Understanding, a program of civic eduction aimed at reducing prejudice and encouraging action on social issues. The program, sponsored by the National Conference of Christians and Jews and other groups, was twice offered on television with more than 8,000 persons formally enrolled in viewing-discussion groups. In 1969, Dr. Robinson was awarded the WTMJ-TV Public Service Award for "distinguished service to the community through broadcasting."

He is an active layman in his church and a student of Bible and Church history. He has taught adult classes in several cities on the Bible and teaching in the Sunday School. His book, *Teaching the Scriptures: A Study Guide for Bible Students and Teachers* is now in its sixth edition. In addition to articles in religious publications, he has written for such professional journals as *Adult Education, Adult Leadership,* and *Journal of Extension.* He is author of *An Introduction to Dynamics of Group Leadership* and *Group Dynamics for Student Activities,* and has a chapter in *Redefining the Discipline of Adult Education.*